MW01087531

CELAN STUDIES

MERIDIAN

Crossing Aesthetics

Werner Hamacher

& David E. Wellbery

Editors

Translated by Susan Bernofsky
with Harvey Mendelsohn

Edited by Jean Bollack
with Henriette Beese,
Wolfgang Fietkau,
Hans-Hagen Hildebrandt,
Gert Mattenklott, Senta Metz,
and Helen Stierlin

Stanford
University
Press

———————

Stanford,
California
2003

CELAN STUDIES

Peter Szondi

Stanford University Press
Stanford, California

Celan Studies was originally published in German in 1972 under the
title *Celan-Studien*, © 1972, Suhrkamp Verlag.

"The Poetry of Constancy: Paul Celan's Translation of Shakespeare's
Sonnet 105," translated by Harvey Mendelsohn, is reprinted by per-
mission of the publisher from *Theory and History of Literature*, vol. 15:
Peter Szondi, *On Textual Understanding and Other Essays*
(Minneapolis: University of Minnesota Press, 1986), pp. 161–78.
© 1986 by the University of Minnesota. All rights reserved.

Other English translation © 2003 by the Board of Trustees of the
Leland Stanford Junior University

Library of Congress Cataloging-in-Publication Data
Szondi, Peter.
   Celan studies / Peter Szondi.
      p.   cm. — (Meridian)
   ISBN 0-8047-4401-7 (alk. paper) — ISBN 0-8047-4402-5 (pbk. : alk.
paper)
   1. Celan, Paul—Criticism and interpretation.   I. Title.
II. Meridian (Stanford, Calif.)
   PT2605.E4 Z843   2003
   831'.914—dc21   20022010298

Original Printing 2003

Last figure below indicates year of this printing:
12   11   10   09   08   07   06   05   04   03

Typeset by BookMatters in 10.9/13 Adobe Garamond

Contents

Foreword

Jean Bollack

Writing a book about Paul Celan was an idea Peter Szondi had been talking about for years, but the project did not take on a concrete form until the beginning of 1971, when he had completed the first two essays included in the present volume. "I have written an article," he wrote to me on December 29, 1970, "on Paul's translation of Shakespeare's Sonnet 105. I think it isn't bad. Very much influenced by Jakobson, Derrida, and Benjamin." Immediately after this (between January 16 and February 1, 1971), Szondi wrote "Lecture de 'Strette'" ("Reading 'Engführung'"), the first long text he'd ever written directly in French. This essay fulfilled a promise he had made to the poet himself on the occasion of their last meeting, on March 17, 1970. Celan had suggested to Jacques Derrida that he commission an essay by Szondi for his journal *Critique*, which was interested in publishing something on Celan's work. Szondi later related how sad Celan had been on the day of this conversation, having brought the matter up himself; he was afraid Szondi would now have to regard this article—which he'd have wanted to write in any case—as a task, an obligation.

From this point on, Szondi became so absorbed in the project that he deferred the publication of two other volumes he'd been working to complete: *Poetik und Geschichtsphilosophie I* and above all *Lektüren und Lektionen*. "The Poetry of Constancy" was originally to have been the final essay in the second of these. The book would have been framed by Shakespeare, with an early miniature, "On a Line from *Romeo and Juliet*," at the beginning and the longer work of linguistic analysis and language philosophy at the end. Removing the second of these two texts would have destroyed the volume's balance.[1]

But Celan's poems had occupied Szondi for many years—they spoke to him more strongly and seemed to him more important than the work of any other contemporary poet. He also felt warmly toward the poet himself and was eager to support him. It was in his company that I met Paul Celan for the first time, in 1959. The concern Szondi clearly felt for him in no way diminished his respect and admiration. On several occasions, he stepped in to counter the attacks being made on Celan during this period.[2]

As early as 1961, Szondi had treated the poems "Sprachgitter" and "Engführung" in a seminar on modern poetry at the Freie Universität in Berlin.[3] When he was invited to give a paper at a conference on German literature in 1963, the interpretation of the poem "Blume" was one of the topics he proposed to the organizers. And these were the poems he intended to use as the basis for a lecture designed for radio broadcast to a much wider audience on the comprehensibility of modern poetry. There is no doubt that Celan's death produced the sense of urgency with which he worked to bring these projects to completion. But each of the essays collected in this volume—and it is this that accounts for their significance—reflects Szondi's lifelong engagement with Celan's poetry.

Szondi had already decided on a structure for the volume. As he wrote to me on February 8, 1971:

I have decided to write a little book about Paul. It will be composed of five studies: (1) "Blume" (*Sprachgitter*), (2) "Engführung," (3) The translation of Shakespeare's Sonnet CV, (4) "Es war Erde in ihnen" (*Niemandsrose*), (5) "Wintergedicht"—Celan's stay in Berlin. In this last article, I will attempt to give all the details that would be of use in understanding the poem ("Du liegst im großen Gelausche") about Rosa Luxemburg and Liebknecht, showing to what an extent it is necessary to know the details to understand the late poems. So: an anti-reading, but with good reason.

This sequence has been preserved, except that the brief sets of notes on "Blume" and "Es war Erde in ihnen"—all we have of these projected essays—have been printed separately from those that were written out. These five essays are listed in Szondi's notebook in the same order, along with the projected number of pages in each of the as yet unwritten pieces: fifteen for "Blume," twenty for "Es war Erde in ihnen," and ten for "Eden" (along with the sixty for "Engführung" and the forty for the sonnet translation).[4] We cannot know whether or not the final version of "Eden" was to have been more extensive than the one we have. In any case, one copy of the final typescript ends with a penciled-in ellipsis. This has been reproduced here, which is surely fitting.

On this page of the notebook, the words *Es war* and *in ihnen* have been crossed out, suggesting that Szondi had decided to use the title "Erde" for his essay; similarly, he crossed out the title "Wintergedicht" and replaced it with "Eden," which corresponds to the title on the corrected typescript. (The photocopy of the typescript bears what was no doubt the essay's original title, "Eden Berlin.") For the planned German version of "Lecture de 'Strette,'" Szondi had first intended to use the title "Engführung" (meaning "stretto," but also, literally, "leading into the strait"); he then changed this to "In die Enge geführt" (Led into the strait), and finally "Durch die Enge geführt" (Led through the strait). These various titles appear in two different drafts of the table of contents for *Lektüren und Lektionen* dating from the beginning of 1971, when Szondi had assembled the essays for this volume, but hadn't yet conceived of *Celan-Studien* as a separate publication. This also is when the essay acquired its subtitle: "Versuch über die Verständlichkeit des modernen Gedichts" (Study on the comprehensibility of the modern poem).

The essay on Shakespeare's sonnet was originally to have appeared in the special issue of *Études Germaniques* (no. 3, 1970) devoted to Celan, but Szondi was unable to meet the deadline.[5] He considered reprinting the article he had written more than a decade earlier defending Celan against the plagiarism charges ("Anleihe oder Verleumdung? Zu einer Auseinandersetzung über Paul Celan" (Borrowing or slander? On a disagreement concerning Paul Celan),[6] but soon decided there was no sense reviving this unlovely episode. As he wrote to Claude David on July 3, 1970, "as for myself, not long after writing to you, I said to myself that it would be better not to return to this affair."

(Paris, June 1972)

Translator's Note

Jean Bollack's 1972 introduction to Peter Szondi's *Celan Studies* leaves unspoken the painful fact that would have been obvious to its readers at the time it first appeared: Bollack was editing his friend's book because Szondi himself had not lived to do so, dead of suicide in the fall of 1971. The exact date of Szondi's death is not known; his body was found in a lake called Halensee on the outskirts of Berlin weeks after he was reported missing on October 8. By taking on the task of preparing Szondi's manuscript for publication, Bollack was bringing to "completion" a project he had followed from its beginnings—it was even he who had worked together with Szondi on preparing the French manuscript of "Lecture de 'Strette'" for publication. His service to Szondi echoes that performed by Szondi himself after the death of Paul Celan on April 20, 1970: scholarship as a tribute, a memorial.

The volume *Celan-Studien*, which Bollack edited together with a number of assistants (Henriette Beese, Wolfgang Fietkau, Hans-Hagen Hildebrandt, Gert Mattenklott, Senta Metz, and Helen Stierlin) contains only one finished essay that was entirely the product of Szondi's pen: the study of Celan's Shakespeare translation "Poetry of Constancy—Poetik der Beständigkeit: Celans Übertragung von Shakespeares Sonett 105," first published in *Sprache im technischen Zeitalter* 37 (1971), 9–25. "Reading 'Engführung,'" published as "Lecture de 'Strette'" in *Critique* 288 (May 1971), 387–420, was translated by the editors from Szondi's French, and "Eden" remained a fragment.

In particular, the incompletion of "Eden" requires some comment. While it is impossible to say how much further Szondi would have taken his reading of Celan's poem "Du liegst im großen Gelausche," it is quite clear that he did not finish writing out everything he had planned. Among his notes for the essay (see Appendix A), one finds the observation that the poem's last lines represent a return to the beginning of the poem in terms of both rhyme and verb tense (he links the use of the imperative and the future). No such comment can be found in the current version of the essay. It is also impossible to imagine that Szondi's completed analysis would have had nothing to say about the identity of the "you" addressed in the first word of the poem and the relationship between this "you"'s actions and the ultimate silence of the Landwehrkanal invoked in the last lines. Szondi's notes contain two versions of the observation: *Darüber, daß nichts stockt, stockt das Gedicht. Daß nichts stockt, macht das Gedicht stocken* ("The fact that nothing stops makes the poem stop short"). The English word "stop" is a poor cousin to the more expressive *stocken*, which implies being shocked to a standstill, unable to go on. The three dots at the end of "Eden" are themselves a sort of *Stocken*.

The title of the essay "Reading 'Engführung'" is a translation of Szondi's original French title, rather than that of the unrealized German version: "Durch die Enge geführt" (Led through the strait), a phrase taken from the end of the essay. Szondi produced his reading of the poem not only in French, but on the basis of its French translation by Jean Daive ("Strette"), referring only occasionally to the German text. Those passages of his essay devoted specifically to the translation have been relegated to the endnotes.

In all three essays, all notes are Szondi's unless otherwise indicated. Material in square brackets was added to Szondi's notes by Jean Bollack (JB), Harvey Mendelsohn (HM), or myself (SB). Added footnotes are indicated by initials only.

Finally, a note on the translations of Celan's poems used in this volume: While a number of English translations of the poems discussed by Szondi in these essays have appeared in recent years, notably in John Felstiner's *Selected Poems and Prose of Paul Celan* (New York: Norton, 2001), I have passed over them in favor of Michael Hamburger's older renderings of "Blume" and "Es war Erde in ihnen" in *Poems of Paul Celan* (New York: Persea, 1980). Hamburger's translations of these two poems, while surpassed by Felstiner's in certain respects, follow the syntax and semantics of the original with a rigor that makes them particularly well suited to supporting Szondi's analyses. The translations of "Du liegst im großen Gelausche" and "Engführung" are my own, the latter heavily indebted to both Hamburger and Felstiner.

(Berlin, October 2001)

CELAN STUDIES

§1 The Poetry of Constancy: Paul Celan's Translation of Shakespeare's Sonnet 105

Shakespeare's Sonnet 105, a poem about the virtues of the author's young friend and, simultaneously, a poem about the poetic writing that extols them, ends with the couplet:

> Fair, kind, and true, have often lived alone,
> Which three till now, never kept seat in one.

Celan's translation of this sonnet concludes with the lines:

> "Schön, gut und treu" so oft getrennt, geschieden.
> In Einem will ich drei zusammenschmieden.[1]

Beauty, goodness, and fidelity are the three virtues that the poet ascribes to his friend in the preceding quatrains, and it is to their expression that he wishes to confine his writing, indeed, even its vocabulary. Whereas in these stanzas Shakespeare speaks not only of his friend, but also of his own love and of his own songs, the final couplet is devoted entirely to the three virtues, which are granted an independent life through the device of personification. Yet this independent life is accorded to beauty, goodness, and fidelity only so that the poet may affirm that their separation, which previously was the rule, is henceforth overcome. The "till now" of the dispersion of "fair, kind, and true" is the history of humanity until the appearance of W. H., who is celebrated in the majority of Shakespeare's sonnets. The last two lines of Celan's translation say something different. They do not contrast the long separation of the three "virtues" with the place in which they finally have all come together. The union of "fair, kind, and true" is due not to the appearance of the friend, but to a literary work, to the future work of the poet, who intends to "forge" the three "together" (*zusammenschmieden*). If Shakespeare's concluding lines are silent about the friend, this is only in order to invoke him all the more strikingly through the negation "never" and above all through the sonnet's inconspicuous last word, "one," which is a circumlocution for him in whom "fair, kind, and true" have taken up common residence. In contrast, Celan's *in Einem* ("in one"), in which the poet "intends to forge together fair, kind, and true," is not "the one *person*" (der *Eine*) extolled by the poem, but "the one *thing*" (das *Eine*), most probably the *one* image that the poet sketches of him, if indeed it is not the unity of the poem, which has entirely absorbed its subject matter. To be sure, in the three quatrains of the Shakespearean sonnet, the poet speaks so explicitly about his work ("my songs and praises," "my verse," "my invention"—in the third line of each quatrain) that, despite the emphatic silence of the concluding couplet, we may interpret the "now," before which moment "fair," "kind," and "true" were separated, as being simultaneously the "now" of Shakespeare's composition of the poem. That the place where beauty, goodness, and fidelity unite could be the friend as well as the poem about him is an ingenious piece of ambiguity based on the relationship between friend and poem established by other poems in the sonnet cycle. In contrast, we may note the explicitness and pathos evident in Celan's translation, in which the poet, through the image of the "forging together," claims that what Shakespeare expresses in the form of a description—and what is linked with the act of its being described only inasmuch as it is a *described* reality—is the product solely of his own will, the result of his poetic activity alone.

The same approach that characterizes Celan's version of the final two lines is a decisive element of his entire translation of Shakespeare's Sonnet 105:

> Let not my love be called idolatry,
> Nor my beloved as an idol show,
> Since all alike my songs and praises be
> To one, of one, still such, and ever so.
>
> Kind is my love to-day, to-morrow kind,
> Still constant in a wondrous excellence,
> Therefore my verse to constancy confined,
> One thing expressing, leaves out difference.
>
> Fair, kind, and true, is all my argument,
> Fair, kind, and true, varying to other words,
> And in this change is my invention spent,
> Three themes in one, which wondrous scope affords.
>
> Fair, kind, and true, have often lived alone,
> Which three till now, never kept seat in one.[2]

> Ihr sollt, den ich da lieb, nicht Abgott heissen,
> nicht Götzendienst, was ich da treib und trieb.
> All dieses Singen hier, all dieses Preisen:
> von ihm, an ihn und immer ihm zulieb.
>
> Gut ist mein Freund, ists heute und ists morgen,
> Und keiner ist beständiger als er.

In der Beständigkeit, da bleibt mein Vers geborgen,
spricht von dem Einen, schweift mir nicht umher.

"Schön, gut und treu," das singe ich und singe.
"Schön, gut und treu"—stets anders und stets das.
Ich find, erfind—um sie in eins zu bringen,
sie einzubringen ohne Unterlaß.

"Schön, gut und treu" so oft getrennt, geschieden.
In Einem will ich drei zusammenschmieden.

In the first quatrain, Celan's use of the active voice leads
to the introduction of the poet's own activity into the subject matter, even though the translation, too, appears to
have only the friend in view. The substantival infinitive
forms of the verbs (*Singen*, "singing," and *Preisen*, "praising,
extolling") replace the corresponding substantives ("my
songs and praises"). Where the passive form "be called" appears in the original, in Celan's version, the poet speaks of
what he himself is doing (the sequence of lines 1 and 2 is re-
versed). And this impression is strengthened by repetition,
specifically by the preservation of lexical identity (*treib/
trieb*, "do/did"), coexisting with morphological difference
(present tense, imperfect tense), as well as by the rhyme on
zulieb ("for the love of").

In the second quatrain, the poet's activity comes to the
fore, since the translator, using both syntax and semantics
to achieve his effect, assigns a more active function to a
verse that is already personified in Shakespeare. In this way,
he also intensifies the personification of his own work,
which increasingly takes the place of the person extolled by
Shakespeare. Celan renders "my verse to constancy confined," as *a bleibt mein Vers geborgen* ("there lies my verse
sheltered") and "leaves out difference" as *schweift mir nicht
umher* ("does not wander round about").

Finally, in the third quatrain, the poet's more active role, the result of the specific accumulation of verbs referring to his own doings (*Ich find, erfind*—"I discover, invent" for "is my invention spent"; *zu bringen, einzubringen*—"to bring, to harvest") is supplemented by greater semantic specification. Thus, "is all my argument," originally a standard rhetorical phrase, is rendered as *das singe ich und singe* ("that [is what] I sing and sing"), preparing the reader for the repetitions to come in lines 11 and 12.

It may seem that the main point involved here is a shift in accent from the person who is being praised to the act of praising or composing. What we are actually dealing with, however, is more than merely the "bolder display" (*das kühnere Exponieren*, as Hölderlin expressed it in connection with his translations of Sophocles)[3] of a theme already present in the original, in which, however, it is entirely subordinate to the themes of the "fair friend"[4] and the poet's love for him. The relationship of Celan's translation to the original can be appropriately described neither as a change in thematic interest or style nor as the kind of change that, according to the tenets of traditional theories of translation, would be pertinent in judging the fidelity and success of the translation. Rather, the movement from original to translation is a change in what Walter Benjamin, in his essay "The Task of the Translator," calls "intention toward language" (*Intention auf die Sprache*).[5] Where a translation not only may, but should differ from the original is in its mode of signification (*Art des Meinens*).[6] The concept of *significatio* pertains to the structure of language, to a relationship whose two members, however, should not be assigned fixed names, since such names always imply a specific relationship between the two, that is, a precise conception of the structure of signification in language. Michel Foucault calls the two elements of this relationship simply "words and things"—a formula that serves as the title of the book in which he interprets the historical change in this relationship as a change in the epistemological "conditions of possibility" governing the specific historical forms assumed by the various "human sciences."[7] Any less general notion would hinder the discovery of the relevant mode of signification, and this would be a serious loss, since it is always this mode that constitutes the historicity of a given linguistic constellation and thus also the goal of philological understanding.[8] Accordingly, a translation does not primarily indicate the historical state of a language (indeed, primarily, it does not indicate this at all); it gives evidence, rather, of the use of language. The translation points not so much to a definite linguistic state as to a definite conception of language. Thus, Benjamin saw the legitimacy, indeed, the necessity of translating as lying in the different intentions toward language and modes of signification displayed by an original text and its translation. This very difference, moreover, invalidates the premises underlying debates over the issue of fidelity versus freedom in translating.

The way in which Celan's mode of signification differs from Shakespeare's can be gathered by comparing the concluding couplet of Sonnet 105 as it stands in the original and in the translation:

> Fair, kind, and true, have often lived alone,
> Which three till now, never kept seat in one.

> "Schön, gut und treu" so oft getrennt, geschieden.
> In Einem will ich drei zusammenschmieden.

The theme in both versions is the separation of the three "virtues" and their unification, the two states being contrasted in the antithetical structure of the couplet. The difference in intention toward language at work in Celan's version and in Shakespeare's text can be inferred from the way Celan expresses the dispersion, as well as the contrast between this dispersion and the ensuing union. In translating "have often lived alone" by *so oft getrennt, geschieden* ("so often separated, divided"), he enriches the discursive mode of expression with another whose poetic energy overwhelms discursiveness. What traditional stylistic criticism would consider as a varied repetition used for emphasis—*getrennt, geschieden*—serves here to express the caesurae between "Schön, gut und treu" in other than simply a lexical manner. Modern linguistics has conceptualized what the reader of earlier times could have perceived in analyzing the impression made on him by a phrase like *getrennt, geschieden*, if—and that is the real question—such a turn of phrase and such an intention toward language appeared at all *before* the advent of modern literature. If it is true that the understanding of language consists primarily in making distinctions, in registering "distinctive features," then the phrase *getrennt, geschieden* is not so much an instance of varied repetition as it is, when spoken aloud as *ge-trennt, ge-schieden*, the union of the common prefix *ge* with two different, although synonymous lexemes, *trennt* and *schieden*. Understanding, which depends upon distinctions, sees intended meaning less in the literal sense of separating and dividing than in the caesura, which splits the word *geschieden* into two parts, by virtue, on the one hand, of the identity of the prefix, and, on the other, of the phonological quasi-identity (the paronomasia) of *schieden* and its rhyme word, *schmieden*. This separation of *ge* and *schieden* may be seen as a metadiscursive representation of the separation of "*Schön, gut und treu.*"

The final rhymes of the English and German versions

display a similar phenomenon. The opposition appearing in the original—"lived alone/kept seat in one"—is, of course, reproduced in the translation, namely, in the opposition of separating and dividing, on the one hand, and forging together, on the other. Nevertheless, it is clear that in the German version, the opposition is conveyed not only through lexical means, but also through the difference between *schieden* ("divided") and *schmieden* ("forged"). Just as understanding, sensitive to distinctions, perceives *geschieden* coming after *getrennt* as *ge-schieden*, so, too, does it register the difference between *geschieden* and *zusammenschmieden* as the minimal consonantal variation of the rhymed syllables *schieden* and *schmieden*. The normative identity of the rhymed words, which in the German text starts from the last stressed vowel (*-ieden*), is reinforced by the *sch* sound, yet this identity is disrupted by the variation arising from the *m* sound in *schmieden* (inserted between the *sch* sound and the rhymed syllable (*-ieden*) and anticipated by the separable prefix *zusammen*). Thus, the metadiscursive realization of both the separation and union of the three "virtues" consists in this minimal variation, the near-identity of *schieden* and *schmieden*. In other words, the opposition is expressed by its own antithesis, paronomasia. This device, employed in the rhyme of the final couplet, enables the poem's language to go beyond the dimension of meaning and *speak* the opposition, instead of expressing it (which would represent a recourse to the literal sense), and it can do this all the more so since the only difference, except for the context (*zusammen*, "together"), between the paronomasia and total homonymy lies in the consonant.

The mode of signification that is documented here and that stamps Celan's translation throughout may be contrasted with the mode found in Shakespeare, which likewise exploits the possibilities offered by rhyme, although in a different fashion. In Shakespeare, the opposition is already emphasized—not, however, by near identity, but by relation, namely, between "alone" (derived from "all one") and "one." Unlike Celan's, this contrastive technique, which is confined to the lexical and etymological realm, is incapable of generating a determinate negation of discursiveness, that is, of recourse to literal sense. More important, however, is the fact that the etymological relationship between "alone" and "one" remains external to the opposition that the poem is meant to express and in fact does express on the discursive level. Thus, the relationship is an abstract point of manneristic origin. The same may be said with even greater justification of the following paradox: Separateness is evoked by the very word ("alone") that originally reinforced the word expressing union ("one"). These remarks are not meant as criticism,[9] but simply as an indication of a particular mode of signification that may be seen as the basic premise of much of traditional rhetoric. Just as this intention toward language has changed since Mallarmé, so the very *principles* of rhetoric employed in poetry since Mallarmé differ from those of traditional rhetoric. This fact, which has been noticed by only a few authors such as Derrida[10] and Deguy,[11] becomes evident in comparing Shakespeare's Sonnet 105 with Celan's translation.

From the point of view of traditional rhetoric, the sonnet's most ingenious line is no doubt the fifth:

> Kind is my love to-day, to-morrow kind.

This line is constructed in the form of a chiasmus. The mirror symmetry directly opposes "to-day" and "to-morrow" around a central axis, thereby stressing the present-future antithesis.[12] On the lexical level, however, inasmuch as the chiastic sentence structure results in the line's beginning and ending with the same word, "kind," it enables the line to stress the constancy that cannot be affected by the temporal opposition. The chiasmus in this Shakespearean verse is thus scarcely mere ornament; at the same time, however, it runs entirely counter to the specific relationship of language and "content" found in Celan's translation of this line:

> Gut ist mein Freund, ists heute und ists morgen.

The chiasmus can be rendered in German, as was shown by Stefan George, whose translation of the line reads:

> Gut ist heut meine liebe · morgen gut ·[13]

If Celan gives up the chiasmus, it is only so as to allow the sentence itself to speak directly what the chiasmus can express only abstractly and mediated by reflection: constancy. Celan's line flows easily onward, replacing the antithetically constructed line, which can express constancy only when it reaches its end in the retrospective glance of synthesis.[14] It is as if Celan's poem were heedlessly following the course of time, in which the friend's goodness persists as unchangingly as the one occurrence of the word *ists* follows the other, as self-evidently as *morgen* ("tomorrow") follows *heute* ("today"). The difference between Celan's translation and the original is not adequately grasped if one merely notes that the chiasmus is replaced by repetition, as can readily be seen from Celan's German version of the succeeding line:

> Und keiner ist beständiger als er.

In Shakespeare this line reads:

> Still constant in a wondrous excellence.

It appears, though, that Celan does wish to reintroduce the chiasmus when he follows up *Gut ist mein Freund* with *keiner ist beständiger* in the next line. But Celan's chiasmus, distributed over two lines and affecting only parts of these two, lacks the antithesis, which becomes a sign of the intended meaning, that is, of constancy, only when it is surpassed qua antithesis through the repetition of the word "kind." In Celan's version, instead of concluding the first line in a gnomic fashion ("kind is my love to-day, to-morrow kind"), the chiasmus confirms the union of the first line with the second, in which the impression of a constant onward-flowing motion is preserved by the use of the introductory word *und* ("and") and by the repetition of the word *ist* ("is").

What distinguishes Celan's translation from the original, therefore, is not a renunciation of traditional rhetorical figures, but rather a change in basic presuppositions. In other words, his version displays a different mode of signification, and this mode underlies his use of language, both generally and, more particularly, with respect to rhetorical figures, although it can be discovered only by a consideration of the "performance," that is to say, the text itself. As a result, even the type of textual analysis that inquires into these presuppositions may no more dispense with stylistic criticism than rely exclusively on the latter.

From this point of view, repetition appears as the most consistently employed stylistic device of Celan's translation. Naturally, the fact that in his own poetry Celan frequently repeats words and sentences lends weight to the thesis that Celan translated Shakespeare into his own language; in other words, Celan's translations are Celan poems. While both plausible and likely to find a ready welcome, though not necessarily false on that account, such an approach tends to obscure the possible difference in the use of language, that is, in intention toward language, which, according to Benjamin's theory of translation, constitutes the difference between an original text and its translation.[15] Hence, we should pursue the comparison of the two poems further still in order to establish the specific mode of signification that informs Celan's language in his translation of the English sonnet.

Shakespeare's own text contains a large number of repetitions, which Celan always retains, however freely he may proceed in other respects. Thus, in the two introductory lines, he translates the pairs of corresponding terms "love-beloved" and "idolatry-idol"; *zulieb*, which corresponds to *lieb* (l. 1), on the other hand, does not appear until the conclusion of the first quatrain, though it is anticipated by *trieb* as its rhyming word. This deviation from the parallelism of the two introductory lines is made for the sake of a varied repetition in line 2 (*was ich da treib und trieb*—"what there I do and did"), which in both its form and underlying intention toward language recalls line 5 (*Gut ist mein Freund, ists heute und ists morgen*—"kind is my friend, [he] is it today and [he] is it tomorrow"). Celan likewise keeps the slightly modified repetition in lines 6 and 7 ("constant-constancy," *beständiger-Beständigkeit*) as well as the strict repetition of "Fair, kind, and true" in lines 9, 10, and 13. One last repetition in the original is made still more emphatic in Celan's version, namely, that found in the final line of the first quatrain:

> To one, of one, still such, and ever so.

The translation refers, however abstractly, to the "fair friend" a third time:

von ihm, an ihn und immer *ihm* zulieb.

about him, to him, and always for love of *him*.

As in the succeeding line, this type of repetition is qualitatively different from the type we find in Shakespeare; it also serves a different function. What Shakespeare, in the second half of the line, expresses discursively with the words "still" and "ever" is spoken by Celan's line *as* line (with the exception of the word *immer*—"ever"). Unlike Shakespeare's line 4 ("To one, of one/still such, and ever so"), Celan's is not divided into two parts, but rather proceeds in a continuous fashion, due to the lexical periodicity (*ihm-ihn-ihm*) as well as the vocalic periodicity (o-ī-a-ī-u-ī-e-ī-u-ī). Here, as in line 5, constancy is not merely the intended meaning, it characterizes the line itself. To this extent, Celan's language does not speak *about* something, but "speaks" itself. It speaks about things and about language through its very manner of speaking.

In Celan's version, therefore, repetition—the syntagmatic realization of the constancy motif—is not restricted to those passages whose explicit theme is *constancy*, but stamps the sonnet as a whole. Behind the many expressions in the original referring only indirectly to this theme, the translator discerns this same constancy and governs his language accordingly. This is evident from the way he translates "my love" in the first line of the original:

Let not my love be called idolatry,

where he makes the constancy implied in "my love" speak through the identity of the lexeme *treib* ("do") in line 2:

nicht Götzendienst, was ich da treib und trieb.

not idolatry what I do and did.

Furthermore, Celan eliminates the discursive "all alike," which links together "songs" and "praises," and instead introduces these two words by the same phrase:

> All dieses Singen hier, all dieses Preisen

> All this singing here, all this praising.

Celan's intention toward language is no less clear when, in the third quatrain, after the identical first part of the two introductory lines, he repeats a word each time in the second part and also makes the sentence structure hinge on this word, as in line 5 (*Gut ist mein Freund, ists heute und ists morgen*):

> Fair, kind, and true, is all my argument,
> Fair, kind, and true, varying to other words.

> "Schön, gut und treu," das *singe* ich und *singe*.
> "Schön, gut und treu"—*stets* anders und *stets* das.

In place of the word "argument," which itself suggests discursive, rational language, and its no less logical qualifier "all," Celan offers the stubborn repetition of his own action. By setting the words *und singe* after *das singe ich* (three words that completely disregard the content of the English phrase "is all my argument"), he creates a repetition that does not simply say what is expressed in the original by the word "all"; moreover, by reducing *das singe ich* to *singe* through the omission of both subject and object, he hypostatizes, as it were, the poet's action. And this is an action that coincides with the poem instead of being its subject matter, as is the case in Shakespeare.

Even more characteristic is Celan's rendering of the phrase "varying to other words": *stets anders und stets das* ("always different and always that"). Varying means "diversifying by change,"[16] "restating in different words."[17] The expression, a rhetorical term, assumes that word and meaning are different and hence distinguishable. It is for this reason alone that the same thing can be designated by different words; it is for this reason alone that it is possible to vary the words without departing from the intended meaning. Celan's intention toward language, by contrast, may be viewed as the determinate negation of this theoretical linguistic premise. What was a stylistic device in traditional rhetoric, and may well have been employed by writers unaware of the conditions that make its use possible, is here recognized by Celan to be a paradox and inserted into the line as such: *stets anders und stets das.* The continuity is conveyed not merely by the word *stets* itself, but even more by its repetition, while the difference is expressed by the fact that *anders* ("other") is followed by *das* ("that," i.e., that same thing). The paradox itself is maintained in two ways. First, the contradiction between *stets*, on the one hand, and *anders* and *das*, on the other, remains unresolved. Second, and no less important, where one expects to find an answer to the possible question "*Different* from what?" there appears a forceful *das*, which, although introduced by the same word, *stets*, is incompatible with *anders*.

Celan's translation of the next line evinces the same rejection of the traditional conception of language, according to which different signifiers can correspond to the same signified. Indeed, we can sense a desire to abolish the distinction between signifier and signified altogether. In this line, Shakespeare explicitly mentions that *change* (i.e., the replacement of one word by another while the intended meaning remains the same), the premise of which is precisely this traditional conception of language:

And in this change is my invention spent.

Celan refuses to concede that words may be interchangeable in this way, just as he successfully avoids using a word derived from the familiar rhetorical term *inventio* to designate the poet's activity and capacity. Designation is replaced by speaking: *Ich find, erfind.* In linguistic terms, this is one of the boldest passages in Celan's version, surpassed perhaps only by the immediately following one. For here, the repetition of the verb, that is, of the word for the activity, does more than simply convey the activity's constancy (which was its sole function in the case of the expressions *Gut ist mein Freund, ists heute und ists morgen* and *das singe ich und singe*). Furthermore, to understand the phrase *Ich find, erfind*, it is not sufficient to read the expansion of "find" in the repetition (*erfind*) as a delayed translation of "invention," nor should it be viewed as a substitute for the dimension of "change" that Celan refuses to mention explicitly or even to accept as a possible means of expressing variation. To be sure, it is also all that. At the same time, however, with the phrase *Ich find, erfind*, Celan pierces the façade of linguistic performance, that is, of *parole* (speech), making it possible to glimpse the inner workings of the linguistic system, of *langue* (language). (He already did this, although in an incomparably less bold fashion, in line 2: *was ich da treib und trieb*.) What is thereby revealed are parts of the conjugation paradigm, once with respect to tense (*was ich da treib und trieb*) and once with respect to person: *Ich find, erfind* (= *er find*). Admittedly, this reading is not compelling in the first case (the change of tense, accompanied by lexical constancy, has its own function, as was seen above); it becomes so only when the first case is considered together with the second (*Ich find, erfind*). Our interpretation of the second case presupposes that, in this position, the prefix *er* carries the connotation of the personal pronoun *er* ("he"). That it actually does so will perhaps be doubted. We may therefore draw attention to two points. First, in the sequence *Ich find, erfind* (as in line 13: *getrennt, geschieden*), understanding, which is concerned above all with "distinctive features," will depart from the usual pronunciation (*erfind*) to stress the prefix *er,* and this is what makes it possible to defend the second meaning (i.e., of *er* as a personal pronoun). Second, it will be recalled that there are passages in Celan's own poems in which paradigmatic fragments of *langue* obviously mingle with *parole,* as in the introductory poem of the collection entitled *Die Niemandsrose:*

> Ich grabe, du gräbst, und es gräbt auch der Wurm
> and das Singende dort sagt: Sie graben.[18]

> I dig, you dig, and the worm, it digs too,
> and that singing over there says: They dig.

The meaning of this questioning of *parole* through the introduction of nonactualized or only partially actualized *faits bruts* of *langue*—a technique that is a constitutive element of the most recent, so-called concrete poetry—becomes evident as soon as we recognize the motivation behind Celan's specific intention toward language, which emerges ever more clearly from the examples analyzed. With this end in view, let us analyze one last instance of varied repetition. At the beginning of the third quatrain, Shakespeare states that he wishes to express the theme of "Fair, kind, and true," which is to be the sole theme of his writing, exclusively by means of varying words; he then continues:

> And in this change is my invention spent,
> Three themes in one, which wondrous scope affords.

Celan translates these lines as:

> Ich find, erfind—um sie in eins zu bringen,
> sie einzubringen ohne Unterlaß.

The passage *sie in eins zu bringen,/ sie einzubringen* is probably the one in which Celan's method of translating lies most open to criticism, the one in which it takes the most liberties. Here, more easily than anywhere else in his German version of Shakespeare's sonnet, we can perceive the specific intention toward language underlying this translation from beginning to end. Celan, as we have seen, does not allow the poet to speak of his own inventive gifts; similarly, he forbids the poet to mention the *scope* of his poetry writing or to call it "wondrous." These words are replaced by two half-lines: *um sie in eins zu bringen* and *sie einzubringen.* Each has its specific content, which can be expressed by other words. The first, the "bringing into one" (which translates "Three themes in one"), should be understood as the union of *"Schön, gut und treu"*—as the poetic mimesis of that union embodied in the friend. The "Three themes" are "One thing" (l. 8). Celan, to be sure, mentions only the unity, the uniting, and not the threefold nature of the manifest reality, which, in Shakespeare, is taken for granted. And his *sie* ("they") refers to the group *"Schön, gut und treu,"* which (in contrast to the practice of many critical editions) also appears each time in inverted commas in the English text printed along with Celan's version,[19] with the result that this group is presented as a quotation, that is, as a verbal entity, not as something real. Thus, the grouping of the virtues, which, in Shakespeare, serves, in however fictive and fictionalized a manner, as the point of departure of the poet's activity, disappears in Celan's text in two respects: It loses both its threefold nature and its existence as something real.

The second half-line *sie einzubringen* ("to bring them in," i.e., to harvest them) cannot be understood as a translation of a specific passage of the original. Once again, what is meant is the act of poetic composition. As metaphor, it would have to be linked with the imagery of a harvest or vintage. If one assumes that the term corresponding to the implicit "whither" of the "bringing in" or harvesting is the poem itself, then the resolution of the metaphor may be seen in the "putting into practice" [i.e., of something in a work of art = *Ins Werk Setzen*]. But such an analytic reading, dependent on "retranslation," is overwhelmed by the wave arising from the paronomasia of *sie in eins zu bringen / sie einzubringen* ("to bring them into one / to bring them in"). Unlike the case of the rhyming pair in the final couplet (*schieden / schmieden*), here the paronomasia is not confined to a portion of a word, but encompasses an entire syntagma. The sequence *sie in eins zu bringen, / sie einzubringen* also differs from the other paronomasia by the fact that it does not stand in the end-rhyme position; the concordance of sounds is therefore not borne by any schema, but strikes the reader unprepared. These differences, however, constitute merely the preconditions for the one crucial difference, and it is the latter that allows us to grasp the specific character of the passage and thereby the particular motivation of Celan's intention toward language, a motivation that is manifest throughout his translation.

By rhyming *zusammenschmieden* with *geschieden*, Celan brings together two signifiers that not only are different, but that have opposite signifieds ("separate"/"join"). He expresses the opposition perhaps even more forcefully through the phonological near-identity, the paronomasia, than through the semantic opposition *e contrario*. In this way, in each case, he subverts the normative conception of the correspondence of the signifieds to the signifiers, the latter of which are assumed to mirror the diversity of the former. (Polysemy is equally the scandal of semiotics and the fundamental fact of poetics.) Now, in contrast to the paronomasia of the final rhyme, the paronomasia of the two syntagmata *sie in eins zu bringen* and *sie einzubringen* is determined not simply by the partial difference between the signifiers *eins* ("one") and *ein* (= *hinein*, "in"), but also through the identity of the signifieds, insofar as Saussure's distinction is at all meaningful and appropriate in the context of Celan's use of language, which seems to be the same sort that has been distinctive of modern poetry since Mallarmé.[20] *Ineinsbringen* ("bringing into one," i.e., uniting) and *Einbringen* ("bringing in") do not normally mean the same thing, any more than do "joining" and "putting into practice," yet, for Celan, to put into practice in a work of art is to unite. The paronomasia of the passage under discussion shows this, and it is suggested by a reading of the German version of the sonnet as a whole. Here we can plainly see Celan's intention toward language and the poetics of his translation. Its program is formulated in the line that renders Shakespeare's

> Therefore my verse to constancy confined

as

> In der Beständigkeit, da bleibt mein Vers geborgen

> In constancy, there lies my verse sheltered.

Constancy, the theme of Shakespeare's sonnet, becomes for Celan the medium in which his verse dwells and that impedes the flow of his verse,[21] imposing constancy upon it. Constancy becomes the constituent element of his verse, in contrast to Shakespeare's original, in which constancy is sung about and described by means of a variety of expressions. Celan's intention toward language, in his version of Shakespeare's Sonnet 105, is a realization of constancy in verse.[22]

We have already seen numerous examples of the recurrence of the same elements and of the creation of similarities that resist the changes wrought by the lapse of time, but the catalogue is not yet complete. Constancy is also conveyed on other linguistic levels than those considered so far. For example, Celan refrains from using enjambment in his translation, whereas he does employ it in his own poetry and also in others of his translations of Shakespeare's sonnets (as does Shakespeare himself). Where this device appears in the original text:

> Since all alike my songs and praises be
> To one, of one, still such, and ever so,

Celan inserts a colon in order to mark the limit of the line:

> All dieses Singen hier, all dieses Preisen:
> von ihm, an ihn und immer ihm zulieb.

In another instance, he replaces a comma (or perhaps a dash)[23] by a period and thereby turns the anaphorically linked lines 9 and 10 into two that are merely juxtaposed:

> Fair, kind, and true, is all my argument,
> Fair, kind, and true, varying to other words,

> "Schön, gut und treu," das singe ich und singe.
> "Schön, gut und treu"—stets anders und stets das.

Whereas in the original text, this pair of lines ends with a comma, Celan interrupts this stanza with a period, as he already did in the first and second stanzas and will do in the couplet as well. (None of Shakespeare's three quatrains consists of more than a single sentence.) It is only in those lines that follow the ones just quoted and that form the most precarious passage of the entire translation that one could speak of enjambment. This is with the appearance of the paronomastic sequence *um sie in eins zu bringen, / sie einzubringen*, which does not stop at the end of the line, although, admittedly, the effect of the enjambment is essentially canceled due to internal repetition.

The syntactic constancy, that is, the regular recurrence of the lines as individual sentences, goes still further: It represents a deviation from the original, indeed, a determinate negation of the latter's way of shaping language. The syntactic subordination, the hypotaxis, of the original poem disappears, and along with it the argumentative and logical style. At the turning points of the quatrains and the couplet, Shakespeare places now causal conjunctions (or adverbs):

> v. 3 *Since* all alike my songs and praises be
> v. 7 *Therefore* my verse to constancy confined;

now the conjunction "and" used consecutively:

> v. 11 *And* in this change is my invention spent;

now a relative pronoun:

> v. 14 *Which* three till now, never kept seat in one.

Celan eliminates these connective words. His sentences are not constructed either to refer to each other or to be subordinate to one another. Celan's translation is profoundly marked by the principle of parataxis, in the literal sense as well as in a broader sense similar to the one Adorno introduced in connection with Hölderlin's later poetry.[24]

Furthermore, Celan reduces the sharpness of the division of the fourteen lines into three quatrains and a couplet, even though he does set off the quatrains typographically from each other (in accordance with the Petrarchan sonnet form) and preserve the rhyme scheme.[25] For, in contrast to Shakespeare's procedure, Celan divides every quatrain into two in the middle, either by the sentence structure or by the punctuation. Consequently, in spite of the rhyme scheme, Celan's quatrains approximate a series of couplets, whereas his couplet is assimilated to the quatrains through syntactic division into two equal parts. In the original, we find dissimilar units (three quatrains and a couplet), and these, by virtue of the way the sentence units are interrelated (causal connection between the halves of stanzas I and II and consecutive connection in stanza III) are hypotactically structured (even if, in the strict sense, there are no subordinate clauses in II and III); as a result, they in turn imply inequality. In Celan's translation, on the other hand, the lines are simply set out one after the other, each a unit that, if it is not autonomous, is nevertheless much less heteronomous than the corresponding line of the original. Just as, on the semantic and phonological levels, Celan's language tends to reduce change, difference, and variety to a minimum, so, too, does it strive for syntactic constancy—in this translation more than in any other.

Celan's intention toward language, as revealed by a study of his German version of Shakespeare's Sonnet 105, ought not to be generalized prematurely. Our investigation dealt with but one sonnet. Nevertheless, the realization of constancy in verse, which is the major finding of our analysis, is not merely a feature peculiar to this one translation. Indeed, it accords with Roman Jakobson's definition of the function of poetic language: "The poetic function projects the principle of equivalence from the axis of selection into the axis of combination. Equivalence is promoted to the constitutive device of the sequence."[26] Jakobson's definition is not a description of a poem, but a statement of the principle governing the poetic use of language in the strict sense of the term. This principle can never be fully realized on the linguistic level if the poem is not to be tautological, in other words, if it is to say anything at all. Celan's translation of Shakespeare's Sonnet 105 approaches more closely than any previous poem to the limiting value of a thoroughgoing realization of the principle of the equivalence in the syntagmatic sequence (if one leaves "concrete poetry" aside). This is so not because Celan's poem—and his translation *is* a poem—is more "poetic" than other poems by him or by others (to conclude this would be to misunderstand Jakobson), but because constancy is the theme of his poem, his translation. Of course, it is also the theme of Shakespeare's sonnet, to which, however, the preceding remarks in no way apply. This point brings us back one final time to the difference between the original and the translation, in other words, to the difference between Shakespeare's and Celan's respective intentions toward language.

"Constancy" can be called the theme of Shakespeare's sonnet insofar as it actually deals with that virtue. Shakespeare asserts and praises the constancy of his "fair friend," and he describes his own writing, whose subject matter is to be exclusively his friend's constancy and the poet's celebration of it. Constancy, at the same time, is conceived of as the means by which this virtue is to be celebrated:

> Therefore my verse to constancy confined,
> One thing expressing, leaves out difference.

But it is as a virtue of the poet's composition that "constancy" figures as the subject matter of the poem. Only in the anaphorical (and thus rhetorically consecrated) repetition of "Fair, kind, and true" does constancy enter the poem's very language.

In Celan's version, we find something very different. Consistent with his overall approach, Celan leaves untranslated those passages in which Shakespeare describes his own poem, his own style, and the goal of his writing, or else he translates them so "freely" that they no longer seem to deal with these topics:

> Since *all alike* my songs and praises be

> All dieses Singen hier, all dieses Preisen:

> Therefore my verse to constancy *confined,*
> One thing expressing, *leaves out difference.*

> In der Beständigkeit, da bleibt mein Vers geborgen,
> spricht von dem Einen, schweift mir nicht umher.

> Fair, kind, and true, *is all my argument,*
> Fair, kind, and true, *varying to other words,*
> *And in this change is my invention spent,*
> *Three themes in one, which wondrous scope affords.*

> "Schön, gut und treu," das singe ich und singe.
> "Schön, gut und treu"—stets anders und stets das.
> Ich find, erfind—um sie in eins zu bringen,
> sie einzubringen ohne Unterlaß.

In Celan's version, the poet does not speak of his "argument," his "invention," or his "scope," but instead, the verse is arranged in accordance with the exigencies of this theme and of this objective aim. Nor does the poet affirm that his verse leaves out difference. Rather, he speaks in a language in which differences are simply left out. Celan, writing in the wake of the later Mallarmé and an attentive observer of modern linguistics, philosophy of language, and aesthetics, drew the logical consequence from the Symbolist conception of poetry, in which a poem is its own subject matter and both invokes and describes itself as a symbol. According to Jakobson, there exists a certain kind of constancy that is projected from the paradigmatic axis (of which it is constitutive) into the syntagmatic axis and that distinguishes the poetic sequence from the prosaic in this latter axis. If we accept Jakobson's views, then we may say that in translating a poem whose subject matter is that very constancy, Celan, perhaps without knowing of Jakobson's theorem, replaced the traditional Symbolist poem—which deals only with itself and which has itself as its subject matter—with a poem which does not *deal with* itself, but which *is* itself! He thus produced a poem that no longer speaks about itself, but whose language is *sheltered* in that very place that it assigns to its subject matter, which is none other than itself: It is sheltered "in constancy."[27]

TRANS. HARVEY MENDELSOHN

§ 2 Reading "Engführung"

[1, 1] Verbracht ins
Gelände
mit der untrüglichen Spur:

Deported to the
terrain
with the unmistakable trace:

These are the opening lines of Paul Celan's 1958 poem "Engführung" (Stretto). The difficulties of reading become apparent the moment the poem begins, but at the same time, they show us that the approaches traditionally employed in literary interpretation—particularly when applied to texts said to be obscure—distort both the reading itself and the text being read. One is immediately confronted, unavoidably, yet misleadingly, with the question of what is meant by this "terrain/with the unmistakable trace." The method to which the reader will no doubt have recourse is that of comparing parallel passages, that is, juxtaposing the lines that resist understanding ("terrain/with the unmistakable trace") with other, more accessible lines from Paul

Celan's work containing one or more of these expressions. Even if one can assume an identity of meaning between one or several such expressions in their various contexts (which itself is questionable), and if the interpretation securely arrived at in one of these passages appears to shed light on the word's usage in the line one is struggling to understand, the line will become clear without having been comprehended, because it is what it is only in the one specific usage—a usage that, moreover, is resisting comprehension. This is why we should stop wondering for the moment what is meant by the "unmistakable trace" and instead note that these first three lines do not tell us what it is, although the repeated use of the definite article suggests that the reader does know what "terrain" and "trace" are being invoked. The opening of "Engführung," then, is characterized less by the (potential) meaning of the expressions used in it than by the fact that the reader finds himself being at the same time drawn into a context he does not recognize and treated as though it were familiar to him; or, to be more precise, he is being treated like someone who has no right to know. From the very beginning, the reader has been deported— *verbracht*, "forcibly brought"—to a terrain that is both foreign and strange. Is this the "terrain/with the unmistakable trace"? We do not know, do not yet know. But it has now been established that if these first few lines specify a referent, the reader cannot safely assume they do not refer to him. Here, too, then, we should stop asking ourselves to whom the phrase "Deported to the/terrain/with the unmistakable trace" refers and instead note that this information is being withheld, and that it is precisely this absence of information that lets the reader assume the phrase refers to him (though not necessarily to him alone). And so the opening lines of "Engführung" give us to understand that while it is not true that the poet is addressing the reader directly (as is the case in a great many poems), nor even that the words have anything to do with him, the reader finds himself transported to the interior of the text in such a way that it is no longer possible to distinguish between the one who is reading and what is being read. The reading subject coincides with the subject of reading.

The poem's first three lines, which make up the first stanza, end with a colon, so the reader now expects the lines that follow to contain information about something he doesn't yet know—a not-knowing that is constitutive of his reading of the first lines of "Engführung."

[1, 2]   Gras, auseinandergeschrieben. Die Steine, weiß,
         mit den Schatten der Halme:

         grass, written asunder. The stones, white,
         with the shadows of grassblades:

The ambiguity of these lines makes it grammatically possible for us to read the grass itself, this "grass, written asunder," as what has been deported to the "terrain/with the unmistakable trace."[1] This is not the reading we most prefer, but it is a possible reading nonetheless; in other words, the link between the first two stanzas of the poem is still governed by ambiguity. "Grass, written asunder"—is this the "terrain with the unmistakable trace" or what has been deported to it? This ambiguity, neither a defect nor purely a stylistic trait, determines the structure of the poetic text itself.[2]

In lines 4 and 5, the reader is confronted with a description of the "terrain with the unmistakable trace": "grass, written asunder. The stones, white,/with the shadows of grassblades." The scene is a landscape, but one described as

a *written* landscape. The grass is "written asunder." A traditional *explication de texte*, one based on a traditional notion
of rhetoric, would no doubt say that the grass in this landscape is being compared to written characters and that it is
the analogy between the one and the other (according to
the Aristotelian definition of metaphor) that allows the poet
to say: "grass, written asunder" and the reader to understand that this grass is like something that has been broken
down into letters. It isn't literally a matter of letters—and
what is the poetic text if not the texture of language?—but
of grass. It is the grass that has been "written asunder." In
other words, this grass is also language, and the landscape is
text. It is because the "terrain with the unmistakable trace"
is (also) text that the reader can be deported to it.

One might wonder what this landscape-text is, or, perhaps more modestly: what it is like. The stanza's second sentence seems to provide an answer: "The stones, white . . ."
This is a terrain composed of whiteness, of void, but also of
stones and shadows. Are these stones tombstones, or merely
those hard, lusterless, impenetrable bodies—the forms, both
crumbling and protective, of stars and eyes—that occupy an
important position within Paul Celan's "imaginary universe"?[3] We do not know, and this means quite precisely that
it is not for us to know. What can be known, can be seen, is
the textuality of the terrain. Once the grass has become letter, the white of the stones is also the white of the page—
whiteness itself,[4] interrupted only by the "grassblade" letters,
or, rather, by the shadows they cast. This landscape-text is a
fateful, funereal terrain. One might be tempted to say that
the reader finds himself deported to a landscape dominated
by death and shadow—the dead and their memory. But
once again, such interpretations are precluded by the textuality of a landscape that is not merely the subject of what we

are reading—it *is* what we are reading. This is why the orders issued by the poet—to himself, the reader? no doubt to both—do not serve as an introduction, as they might in poetry of a certain sort. One can receive and follow these orders only once one has been "deported" to the text-terrain.

> [1, 2] Lies nicht mehr—schau!
> Schau nicht mehr—geh!
>
> Read no more—look!
> Look no more—go!

The joint actions of reading and gazing are appropriate to this ambiguous terrain, which is at once text and scene. The first command would substitute the gaze for the reading process, leaving behind the textuality of the landscape so as to consider the landscape in its own right. But the second command, which contradicts, cancels out the first (in a figure essential to "Engführung," as will be seen), replaces the gaze with movement. Does this mean the text being read and the picture being looked at have to give way to reality, permitting the spectator-reader to move forward, "go"? Yes and no. It isn't the fiction of textuality, of poetry, that is being abandoned in favor of reality. It isn't the receptive passivity of the spectator-reader that is being forced to yield to so-called real action, engagement. On the contrary: The text itself is refusing to serve reality, to go on playing the role that has been assigned to it since Aristotle. Poetry is ceasing to be mimesis, representation; it is becoming reality. To be sure, this is a poetic reality: The text no longer stands in the service of a predetermined reality, but rather is projecting itself, constituting itself as reality. Thus, we are no longer to "read" this text nor to "look" at the picture it might be describing. What the poet is asking of both himself and the reader is to move forward, "go," into this terrain that is his text.

Move forward? How, and for what reason?

[1, 3] Geh, deine Stunde
     hat keine Schwestern, du bist—
     bist zuhause. Ein Rad, langsam,
     rollt aus sich selber, die Speichen
     klettern,
     klettern auf schwärzlichem Feld, die Nacht
     braucht keine Sterne, nirgends
     fragt es nach dir.

     Go, your hour
     has no sisters, you are—
     are at home. A wheel, slow,
     rolls out of itself, the spokes
     climb,
     climb on a blackish field, the night
     needs no stars, no one
     asks after you.

The hour that has no sisters, or no longer has any, is one's final hour, the hour of death. Having arrived there, one is "at home." This topos acquires a new meaning in Celan's work. If death is the harbor to which one returns, it is not because life is a journey, but because death, the memory of the dead, lies at the origin of Celan's entire poetic oeuvre. Since his poetry no longer describes "reality," but rather itself becomes reality, the "blackish field" is no longer what his poetry describes, but what it causes to come into being. It is upon this field that it moves forward, writing itself, and it is upon this field the reader moves. At the same time, the substitution of textual reality for textual representation (which ostensibly is at the service of reality) should not be seen as pointing to what is known as aestheticism; rather, it testifies to the poet's determination to respect the reality of death, the reality of the death camps, and not to attempt to use it to produce a poetic tableau. At the same time, he respects the aesthetic reality of his poetry, which is devoted almost exclusively to the memory of the dead.

This reality is characterized by a movement that has no motor but itself: The wheel "rolls out of itself." The region to which one is returning so as to be "at home"[5] seems to have no need of the one moving toward it: The forward motion of the poet-reader is enough to make the spokes of the wheel rise and fall. But it isn't so much that the subject—author or reader—is being pushed aside, replaced by the object that is the wheel. Rather, once the subject is "at home," it ceases to be a subject and enters into the text even more radically than in the opening lines of the poem. As a result, its progression becomes that of the spokes: The subject is no longer the reader or spectator of anything other than itself. It has become a wheel. And in this night, this realm of death that would not exist as such if it were lit up with stars, "no one/asks after you."

These words that end the first section of "Engführung" reappear at the beginning of the second (the poem being composed of nine parts). But this repetition takes a special form. Each time we move to a new section of the poem, we find the final line or lines of the preceding one printed at the right-hand edge of the page, which is otherwise empty—printed either in the same form as before, modified, rearranged or even, in one case, expanded. These reiterated lines come before the beginning, properly speaking, of the new sections:

[II]   Nirgends
                            fragt es nach dir—

Der Ort, wo sie lagen, er hat
einen Namen—er hat
keinen. Sie lagen nicht dort. Etwas
lag zwischen ihnen. Sie
sahn nicht hindurch.

Sahn nicht, nein,
redeten von
Worten. Keines
erwachte, der
Schlaf
kam über sie;

                    No one
                            asks after you—

The place where they lay, it has
a name—it has
none. They did not lie there. Something
lay between them. They
did not see through it.

Did not see, no,
spoke of
words. None
awoke,
sleep
came over them.

What on first reading might suggest the idea of an echo
takes on new significance when we consider the precise
meaning of the musical term "stretto" (from *strictus*). "In a
fugue the stretto is an artifice by which the subject and answer are, as it were, bound closer together, by being made to
overlap" (*Oxford English Dictionary* 2d ed.).[6] The "reprises"

at the beginning of each section, then, are not simple repetition. Rather, the words printed at the right-hand edge of the page are meant to coincide with the entrance that follows them. Their typographical placement reproduces the staggered entrances that are an essential feature of the musical stretto and that give it the sense of urgency indicated in the definition.

This notion of the stretto, insufficient as it might be for defining a poetic text, is the starting point from which one must attempt to understand the composition of Celan's poem. The principle of composition—what is called "stretto" in music—explains the function of the repeated lines and the tightly interwoven ("strict") linkage between the nine sections of the poem. On the other hand, it also presents these sections as voices. This is in fact what they are, and not just in the musical sense:

The first section, in the present tense, posits a subject that is speaking to another: It issues orders ("Read no more—look!/Look no more—go!") and declares that "no one/asks after you."

The second section, dominated by the past tense, is a description that does not involve the "speaking" subject, but instead concerns a "they": The third person plural, then, determines the "voice" of section II.

Among the various fragments of voices scattered among sections III to IX, the third section, in both present and past tenses, introduces direct discourse in the first person ("It is I, I,/I lay between you"), while the fourth section, also combining present and past, resembles the second, except that here it is a matter not of persons, but of the time they pass through or that forms their past ("years./Years, years, a finger/gropes up and down"). The fifth section—which is preceded by (or rather commences at almost the same mo-

ment as) the end of the fourth, itself reprised in inverted
form ("who/covered it up?" becomes "Covered it up/
who?")—reverses the temporal direction of parts I and II
taken together and of part IV taken independently, in other
words, reverses the passage from present to past that constitutes the initial movement of the poem: the act of remembering. Now the path followed by the poem leads us from
the past tense ("Came, came./Came a word, came") to the
present—first to the present of temporal information
("Night./Night-and-night") and then to the imperative
present ("Go/to the eye, the moist one"). We can note, at
this point, that the passage from the fourth section to the
fifth (which stands at the very center of the composition,
given that the final section, printed within parentheses,
reprises the beginning of the poem) marks the turning
point of "Engführung." The sixth section, the longest of the
nine, differs from the first half of the poem (sections I–IV)
in that the speaking subject is no longer addressing itself exclusively to a "you" ("as you/know"), but rather refers to itself and its interlocutor together as "we" ("as we/read in the
book," "How/did we touch/one another—touch with/
these hands?"). This "we" is reprised in the eighth section
("near/our fugitive hands"), while the intervening section
(VII), composed of description and narration ("Nights, unmixed. Circles,/green or blue, red/squares: the/world stakes
its innermost/in the game with the new/hours") dispenses
entirely with personal pronouns. Unlike the first half of the
poem (marked by the sequence: second person singular,
third person plural, first person singular), the second half—
which moreover repeats the new temporal sequence of past
(VI) → present (VIII)—is essentially determined by the
first person plural.

The task now facing us is to grasp the meaning of Celan's

use of the stretto form. It isn't possible to do this without first understanding, that is, *reading* the relationships between the different voices. We say "read," although establishing these relationships is a matter of interpretation, the relationships being not the object, but the result of reading. So not only is there no object (of reading) without a reading subject, without reading—which, as may be unnecessary to point out, by no means implies that reading has the right to create its own object as it sees fit—but since the text exists in the texture of its language, the interpretation will not be introducing anything foreign if it attempts a description of this verbal tissue. The weave in the case of "Engführung" is precisely the composition of different voices that make up the different sections of the poem. Establishing the nature of this fabric involves not only understanding the relationships between the voices (and thus between the various sections of the poem), but also taking into account the fact that these relationships are realized in the text in a manner that is not discursive, but rather, if one may say so, musical: the stretto form. This has the additional consequence that since the relationships between the various sections of the poem determine its progression, since these relationships partake of a construction that imitates musical form, and since, finally, this musical construction has been transposed into a verbal medium and designated by its *name* in the poem's title, this title must be understood as a name (and not merely as a musical term) if we hope to produce a reading—one that will admittedly remain incomplete—of the poem "Engführung."

The first section of the poem deports the subject (author or reader) into a terrain that is simultaneously the terrain of death and that of the text. The subject can be seen advancing into this terrain, apparently without eliciting concern.

The end of this first section ("No one/asks after you—") coincides with the beginning of the second, whose initial
stanza we cite here once more:

> [II, 1] Der Ort, wo sie lagen, er hat
> einen Namen—er hat
> keinen. Sie lagen nicht dort. Etwas
> lag zwischen ihnen. Sie
> sahn nicht hindurch.
>
> The place where they lay, it has
> a name—it has
> none. They did not lie there. Something
> lay between them. They
> did not see through it.

Composing a poem on the model of a stretto (or perhaps
we should say: on the model of a musical form in general)
implies at least partially renouncing the use of discursive expression. This is why it is not only the words and phrases
that must be *read*, but also, and perhaps above all, the relationships created between them by means of repetition,
transformation, and contradiction. In a stretto, this is first
and foremost true of the jointures between the different
voices. These are relationships that can never be established
with certitude, since we are translating from a language that
is neither verbal nor discursive into a language of reading
that is both. But if the language of reading is not to distort
the reading, it cannot substitute a predetermined meaning,
a positive certitude, for something that does not resemble
these things, does not value them. Considering the relationship between I and II, we might assume that in all like-
lihood, the subjects appearing in the past in section II are
the one of whom it is said "No one/asks after you" and one
other person, and that the past referred to is a past being

recollected to (or by) this person who is advancing into the "terrain" that is the poem. In other words, this advance is at the same time a return: "you are—/are at home" (I). The poem's line breaks have a signifying function not only for the sections, but also for individual lines, as is the case throughout Celan's work. This particular line break, reinforced by the repetition of the verb "are," points to what the reading is learning as it goes on. "You are"—we don't yet know whether to expect a further piece of information, linked to this one, that will say more about this "you," or whether the phrase is simply an existence claim. "Are at home"—having now received this supplementary information, we understand that the "you"'s at-homeness is at issue. But we also know (or, more precisely, we read) that it is *also* a matter of existence itself; that *to be* (as we've learned only through this supplementary information) is *to be at home*; and that existence, according to "Engführung," is attained only when one has returned home (to one's origins? one's mother?—Celan's ineradicable memory of his mother's death in a concentration camp). True existence becomes conjoined with nonexistence, or, more precisely, it is existence only when it remains faithful to, when it remembers nonexistence.

Since to advance is to return, the second section evokes a place in the past "where they lay," a place that "has / a name . . . it has / none." This movement—a figure known in rhetoric under the name *correctio* that is, as we have said, essential to the discourse of "Engführung"—must be considered with the greatest care, keeping in mind that even here, the reading subject is given no information about the motifs or the reason for the corrections (which makes them seem close to musical composition and its discourse). What we can now perhaps say is: If the place that has a name does not in fact have one, and if, in this place where they lay, they did not lie down, it is because "Something/lay between them." We don't yet know what this "something" is, only that it is preventing them from seeing (one another?), but in section III, it will begin to speak and proclaim its nature. This is the meaning of the second jointure (between sections II and III).

But before we move on to the self-presentation of what "lay between them," let us read the second stanza of section II:

> [II, 2] Sahn nicht, nein,
> redeten von
> Worten. Keines
> erwachte, der
> Schlaf
> kam über sie.
>
> Did not see, no,
> spoke of
> words. None
> awoke,
> sleep
> came over them.

The persons here referred to have not merely been speaking in or with words: they *redeten von/Worten*, "spoke *of* words," even "talked words."[7] The deficient mode of existence in this place, resulting from the fact that "Something/lay between them," is at the same time a verbal deficiency, a deficiency expressed through the mediation of the word, a deficiency of language itself. These three possible readings should be understood as distinct, but equally legitimate: It is their combination, here as elsewhere, that constitutes the texture of the poem. Also ambiguous is the pronoun *keines* ("none"): It can refer both to the words and to those who speak them. This ambiguity is all the more important for being "denied" in the following lines: "sleep/came over them"—with the quotation marks around "denied" signaling that this ambiguity is simultaneously being denied and not denied, since the movement of the *correctio* is that of Celanian discourse itself. Even more important is the observation that in "None [no word]/awoke," the deficiency characterizes not only the ones who exist and their mode of existence, but also their language, which in "Engführung" is always at the same time existence, reality: the reality of language, of text. It is *because* "None/awoke" that "sleep/came over them."

In the third section, this "something" that "lay between them" (II) speaks:

[III]   Ich bins, ich,
         ich lag zwischen euch, ich war
         offen, war
         hörbar, ich tickte euch zu, euer Atem
         gehorchte, ich
         bin es noch immer, ihr
         schlaft ja.

         It is I, I,
         I lay between you, I was
         open, was
         audible, I ticked to you, your breathing
         obeyed, it is
         I still, and you
         are asleep.

But first we read, at the right-hand edge of the page, not the end of the second section in unchanged form ("sleep/came over them"), but: "Came, came. No one/asks—." The voice of what "lay between them" (II), then, does not begin to speak by declaring itself to be the "sleep" that "came over them" (II); rather, it presents itself (if we "read" the musical jointure) simply as something that "came." This might be sleep, but it might be something else as well. The reduced "repetition" of the end of section II at the "opening" of section III prevents the question of this "something"'s identity from being resolved for the time being (which corresponds to the ambiguity of "None awoke"—words or persons?) This jointure, following the model of the stretto, tells us first of all that this "something" that "lay between them" and will later begin to speak is a thing that arrives, a thing whose essence is this arrival and that arrives upon a "blackish field" where—according to the second part of the "repetition"—"no one/asks" after those to whom this "something" will speak.

What is this "something"? It should be possible to propose an answer without being untrue to the task we set ourselves for this reading: without foregoing interpretation itself (which would be impossible), but avoiding private associations, private readings. This "something," then, calls itself "open" and also "audible." So the "narrative" [*récit*] of the second section is now becoming clear: The ones between whom this something lay "spoke of/words," none of which, however, "awoke" (II). The words are asleep in that they do not speak. The ones who "spoke of/words" are unable to profit from the audibility of what "lay between them." They experience this "something" only as a partition ("They/did not see through it"), rather than perceiving its audibility, its openness, and realizing that it is something that might be entered, a new "field"—given that being is always at the same time word.

This "something" "ticked to you."[8] The action of this "something" consisted of ticking, but it is an action directed toward the persons being referred to: "I ticked *to you*." The verb *ticken*, then, does not signify merely "to make a tick-tock sound." In early-twentieth-century German usage, *ticken* still had the additional, even primary meaning "to touch with a fingertip." An avid reader of dictionaries, Celan—who filled a small notebook with all the words in Jean Paul whose meaning is no longer clear today (*Sprach-gitter* ["speech grille"] for example, used for the title of the volume that concludes with "Engführung")—can be assumed not only to have known this sense of *ticken*, but to have employed it by design, for the sake of its ambiguity. *Ticken* in this passage of "Engführung" means both "to make a tick-tock sound" and "to touch," and the word *ticken wants* to express both things at once, since the two meanings here coalesce into a single one. What is touching, what is ticking, is many things at once: a clock, emblem of time, time itself, temporality. What is "between them," what is "open," "audible" at this final hour ("your hour/has no sisters," I), is nothing other than time: what arrives, what ticks, what wishes to carry along with it the ones it is addressing. Does it succeed?

"Your breathing/obeyed": this audible "something," then, is not actually heard, but it nonetheless manages to touch (with a finger) the activity that is not interrupted by sleep, "breathing." But taking control of their breathing is apparently not enough for the "something" to attain its goal, otherwise the poem would not continue "and [after all] you/are asleep." Let us not forget, even for a moment, that *schlafen* does not signify *only* "to sleep." *Schlafen* is often used euphemistically to mean "to be dead," and here it has the additional meaning "not to hear." If this reading is correct, then it is also possible, perhaps even necessary, to say that "to live" means "to hear"—a hypothesis confirmed

by the equation of "existence" and "word" by the "textual"
character of the reality that "Engführung" imposes on its
reader from the outset ("grass, written asunder").

Thus, one must conclude that what "lay between them"
as they lay there, sleeping upon the "blackish field" that is
death (that death is), non-time—the "something" that,
through the double meaning of *ticken*, appears to be time
(or a certain time, a certain temporality), and that is also
language, word—must have had the chance, by making itself audible to them, to awaken them, that is: to lead them
into existence, give them life. This goal has not been
achieved: "and you are asleep." But the "something"-time-
word ("word" in the emphatic sense) that was "audible" re-
assures us: "it is/I still." "Nothing is lost," one might say,
anticipating a line from the penultimate section of the
poem. And it is in fact this confirmation, this "reprise" of
the end of section III at the right-hand edge of the page,
that begins the fourth section:

[IV]   Bin es noch immer—

    Jahre.
    Jahre, Jahre, ein Finger
    tastet hinab und hinan, tastet
    umher:
    Nahtstellen, fühlbar, hier
    klafft es weit auseinander, hier
    wuchs es wieder zusammen—wer
    deckte es zu?

                   It is I still—

    Years.
    Years, years, a finger
    gropes up and down, gropes
    around:

> seams, palpable, here
> it is split wide open, here
> it grew together again—who
> covered it up?

While the third section contains the discourse of the "something," at once time and word, which appears here in the consolatory affirmation that it still *is*, the fourth section introduces the description or, better: the evocation of what time is, as well as man's commerce with time. We use the word "evocation" because the character of time and of the commerce those who exist have with it is not only being described here, but also—in a privileged manner, even—expressed *in* the discourse itself. The structure of the words, going beyond the semantic level, evokes continuity, infinity, but also the caesuras of inner time created within human beings by the past: memory.

"Years./Years, years"—it is important to know how to read the fact that nothing is actually *said* of this time/duration, that the poet merely names it. And one has to know how to read the fact that it is taken up again, repeated, in the following line, where the name evokes the thing and the repetition its essential character: duration. Since time becomes spatial as soon as one attempts to describe it (always, but particularly in "Engführung"), the "terrain" of memory takes the form of a surface, a vague landscape of valleys and hills lacking any fixed points of reference. A person cannot simply move across it; he has to grope his way along, as if he were only a finger. Perhaps we ought to revert briefly to the traditional discourse of *explication de texte*, in this case the "as if," so as to show to what extent this discourse distorts both what is written and what we are reading. While what we have here is an instance of synecdoche, the part ("a finger") representing the whole (the one remembering), it is in fact crucial to realize that it doesn't matter what this "finger" represents. Nowhere in the stanza is the thing represented by it at issue; in other words, it isn't a matter of representation at all. It is this finger and nothing else that is doing the touching. One can interpret this touching as an act of memory, but the interpretation distorts the text the moment one forgets that the text speaks of *tasten* ("to touch, to grope"), and not of remembering. The "finger," which recalls that other finger implied in *ticken* ("to touch with a fingertip"), establishes a certain affinity between those who exist and time, between those who are sleeping (III) and the one who is ticking: the opening up of inner time. This ticking one, "lost," has tried to become "audible" to the others, to involve them in the search for himself. If the return to the past has not yet taken place, it is perhaps because of what characterizes this past: "seams, palpable, here/it is split wide open, here/it grew together again"—a past heavy with wounds, a traumatic past. For that matter, the time said here to be "open" (III) is simultaneously covered: "who/covered it up?" (IV). The two contradictory attributions are spoken by two different voices: by the voice of the "something"-time (in the third section) and by the voice of the ones who, touching only with a finger, are hesitating to plunge into the opening that is their memory (section IV). In order not to distort the reading by the interpretation (and what we are about to say marks, in a general way, the difference between reading and interpretation), let us affirm that in the fourth section of the poem it is not stated that this "something" has been covered (or even that the "subject" of IV is this "something" that "lay between them," II). All that is given voice to is the question: "who/covered it up?"

This question, reprised in inverse form, leads into the opening of the following section:

[v]   Deckte es
                                    zu—wer?

Kam, kam.
Kam ein Wort, kam,
kam durch die Nacht,
wollt leuchten, wollt leuchten.

Asche.
Asche, Asche.
Nacht.
Nacht-und-Nacht. —Zum
Aug geh, zum feuchten.

                             Covered it
                                    up—who?

Came, came.
Came a word, came,
came through the night,
wished to shine, wished to shine.

Ashes.
Ashes, ashes.
Night.
Night-and-night. —Go
to the eye, the moist one.

This is the central section of "Engführung" (the division of whose parts we can indicate by the formula 4 + 1 + 4). We have now arrived at the turning point of the progression that began in section I: progression in terms of the text being written and progress from the point of view of the reader. This turning point comes about, as we have seen, through the use of tense shifts, the movement from I to IV proceeding from present to past, and that from V to IX, in reverse, from past to present. This movement appears on a smaller scale within the fifth section: The first of the two stanzas is in the past tense, while the second is in the present, as indicated by the invocation that begins it ("Ashes./ Ashes, ashes./Night./Night-and-night") and the final imperative, which is separated by a dash from what precedes it ("Go/to the eye, the moist one").

So when one has "read" the jointure of IV and V and the structure of V as one reads a score, in other words, by analyzing rather than translating them, one discovers the rupture within the question contained in the "reprise" ("Covered it/up—who?") and the abyss that separates the two stanzas this question introduces. This rupture is signaled by the syntactic device of inversion ("who/covered it up?" becomes "Covered it/up—who?")[9] and by the orthographic device of the dash that marks precisely the point of rupture ("Covered it/up—who?"). Ought we to ask ourselves the meaning of this rupture? This would mean abandoning the principle of musical reading. We could do so all the same—after all, the text before us is a poetic work, and our reading makes use of various techniques. But this principle seems to suggest itself here: The rupture needs no interpretation, since the entrance preceded by this fractured question—or more precisely: the relationship between the question and the entrance that follows—itself illumines the rupture's function. (We are using the term "function" rather than "meaning," which pertains to semantics, since we consider the "syntactical" level, in the broad sense of the term, to be the level of composition.) If this entrance ("Came, came./Came a word, came,/came through the night") illumines the function of the rupture within the question, it is only because it cannot serve as a response to the question "who/covered it up?" It is still inconceivable that it should be the *word* that comes, comes because it wishes to shine in this night of sleeping words ("None/awoke," II) that has covered over (*zugedeckt*) the opening of memory. At the same time, saying that this is inconceivable and concluding that the question has been ruptured amounts to affirming that the interrogatory pronoun in the reiterated question ("Covered it/up—who?") is not the same "who?" as the one in the final question of IV ("who/covered it up?") and that in the second question, the pronoun is no longer the subject of the predicate. We don't find this thesis particularly far-fetched or in danger of being false. Though it does become false if one fails to take into account the fact that this "who?" presents itself, despite everything (despite the inversion and the dash) as the subject of the predicate "Covered it up," which it is not. What we have just described, adhering more strictly to the method of musical analysis than to that of *explication de texte*, also strongly resembles the possibility, in musical composition, of replacing a note with what is known as its enharmonic equivalent. The moment one agrees that the "who?" of "Covered it/up—who?" is being presented simultaneously as the subject of the question and cut off from the rest, it takes on a new function as the question corresponding to the answer constituted by the following section ("Came, came./Came a word"). This reading asserts the existence of two different functions and a shift from one to the other—which is precisely what the use of an enharmonic entails. This only serves to confirm our premise that reading "Engführung" demands that one consider not so much the meaning of the words as their function.

As for the rift separating the two stanzas of the fifth section, let us simply note its existence and try to determine its function, rather than translating this structural moment into a discourse on the level of utterance, of meaning. Even a basic reading would acknowledge the presence of a rift between the two stanzas, a radical opposition that includes no form of mediation.[10] Between the universe of the "word" that comes "through the night" wishing to "shine" and that *has* in fact come ("Came, came./Came a word"), on the one hand, and the world of "ashes," on the other, this absolute "night" that knows only itself and is "Night-and-night," we can see only pure opposition, caesura. The function of this caesura is intelligible only in the light of the composition of the poem as a whole, which describes a progression consisting of a departure and a return (from present to past and from past to present), a progression experienced by consciousness as memory. This is an experience that involves a return to the point of departure, but the origin is transformed by the experience itself—an adventure or event that in the end is nothing other than the text of the poem in the process of being realized. Midway along this path, a path not described but followed—*taken*, or more precisely, *opened* by the poem itself—we find a turning point where the two worlds stand in opposition. It is this opposition that makes the experience necessary, an opposition that is resolved only through the advent that is the poem's event, that *is* the poem. To be sure, nothing would be more foreign to Celanian discourse than to speak openly of this opposition. In the poem, it is merely *realized* (if indeed one can speak here of limitation, rather than of going beyond traditional poetic language, which until Mallarmé was principally concerned with representation), *realized* in the confrontation of the two stanzas of the fifth section with one another. The poem forces this confrontation at its own midpoint (since this section is preceded and followed by four sections each), and thus reveals itself to be this progression, rather than making the confrontation a topic for description, representation. The command that ends the second stanza of section V, set off by a dash, is repeated without change, but in a slower rhythm (determined by the three lines in which it unfolds), in the "reprise" at the join-ture of V and VI:

> Zum
>   Aug geh,
>   zum feuchten—

> Go
>   to the eye,
>   the moist one—

This command appears to be addressed to the word of which it is said at the beginning of V that it "Came, came." But in its function as command, it seems also to be recalling the commands from the very first section:

> [1,2] Lies nicht mehr—schau!
>   Schau nicht mehr—geh!

> Read no more—look!
> Look no more—go!

Ordinarily, the command would be understood as addressed either to the word or to the poet/reader. Here, the two terms are not only compatible, but identical, not only because the text is the progression of the poetic act and the reading the progression of the text, but because this progression coincides with the advent ("and/it came," VI) that is realized in the poem.

This identity, which is paradoxical, but stems from the poem's own logic, emerges in the course of the sixth section, which is much longer than the others. One might even say it is characterized by a disconcerting verbosity, so much so that our reading will no longer be able to follow the text of the poem line by line, as it has so far. At the same time, we shouldn't content ourselves with simply acknowledging or even criticizing this verbosity, but instead should seek to understand the reason for it. Which again brings us to the question—in a different form this time—of what role language plays in the poem.

Sleep "came over them" (II, 2). This is, in Hegelian terms, a "bad" nonbeing, one that prevents them from hearing what has come to speak to them and lead them to the opening that is their past—itself a nonbeing, but one without which, without the memory of which, there can be no existence. It is precisely the destination toward which the poem has been leading. The word, too, comes (V). It comes through the night, wishing to "shine." The "moist" eye, the eye full of tears, toward which, at the end of V and in the "reprise" that precedes the sixth section, someone or something is instructed to go—we believe this to be the eye of the beings of whom it is said, near the beginning of the poem, that "Something/lay between them. They/did not see through it. // Did not see, no,/spoke of/words" (II). The sixth section describes what happens to them once the word arrives, or rather, what they do once they are awake and ready to do what is being asked of them: to follow their path through the past to find a reality that will no longer be this wordless nonbeing.

This progression is not the subject of the poem but its movement, and the poem is not the representation of a reality, but is itself reality. What is at stake in section VI, then, is nothing other than the creation of the world, its re-creation through language. So it is not by chance that the first stanza uses quotations to evoke both the cosmogony of Democritus and the theological structure of the world in the work of Dante.[11]

[VI, 1] Orkane.
Orkane, von je,
Partikelgestöber, das andre,
du
weißts ja, wir
lasens im Buche, war
Meinung.

Cyclones.
Cyclones, age-old,
particle flurry, the rest,
as you
know, as we
read in the book, was
opinion.

According to Democritus, the world, like all the things and beings contained in it, results from the "flurry" (*Gestöber*) of atoms. They, along with the void, constitute the basis of the universe, "all else is only opinion."[12] For Celan, this "opinion" becomes the *bad* nonbeing of which we have spoken, the "speaking of words" (II) of which nothing comes. Reading this stanza, we can see that the use of line breaks places the metrical emphasis on words whose importance will become clear only in the second stanza of VI: "you," "we," "was," and "opinion." The combination of these elements in the second stanza allows us to propose a reading of "was opinion":

[VI, 2] War, war
Meinung. Wie
faßten wir uns
an—an mit
diesen
Händen?

> Was, was
> opinion. How
> did we touch
> one another—touch with
> these
> hands?

What was only opinion, language devoid of reality, now stands in opposition to the physical reality of the contact of the hands, the two bodies—something unexplained, if not inexplicable, since the voice asks how this was possible. But the stanza shows the role these two beings will play in re-creating the world through language and with the help of their memory, a re-creation that—as is becoming more and more apparent as our reading progresses—is a task incumbent not on them alone, but on the poem itself. It is no longer a question of "particles" (VI, 1), of atoms. Yet it is a disquieting sign that the voice can wonder how this contact between the hands was able to come about. We are reminded of the "finger" that "gropes up and down, gropes/ around" (IV) in the traumatic past, this finger with whose help the "hands" clasping one another wish to call into existence a new cosmos. The path the word has taken, traveling "to the eye . . . the moist one" (V, 2), the path taken by the ones who, their eyes moist, have set themselves this task, was not the path that should have been taken:

> [VI, 3–4]   Es stand auch geschrieben, daß.
> Wo? Wir
> taten ein Schweigen darüber,
> giftgestillt, groß,
> ein
> grünes
> Schweigen, ein Kelchblatt, es

hing ein Gedanke an Pflanzliches dran—
grün, ja,
hing, ja,
unter hämischem
Himmel.

An, ja,
Pflanzliches.

It was written, too, that.
Where? We
put a silence upon it,
poison-quenched, huge,
a
green
silence, a sepal, there was
a thought of vegetation attached to it—
green, yes,
attached, yes,
beneath a spiteful
sky.
Of, yes,
vegetation.

The heavens are "spiteful" because they have not reached their goal. Rather than gaining possession of the word (that is, existence) and creating their new world at this final hour that "has no sisters" (I), they have introduced "a silence." Once again, the past has been suppressed. For what reason? The poet does not say, and, as our reading of these three stanzas shows, the poem now appears, unlike in earlier sections, to be distancing itself from musical language and embracing a more traditional hermetic discourse. Meanwhile, our reading has itself almost, despite our intentions, begun to fall back on line-by-line paraphrase, *explication de texte*.

But it is still only the text itself that permits us to explain why this failure has occurred—the constellation in which one finds the "thought of vegetation" and the "green silence" to which the thought was "attached." The following two stanzas of the sixth section show us a different possibility, the antithesis of the plant silence.

[IV, 5–6] Ja.
　　　Orkane, Par-
　　　tikelgestöber, es blieb
　　　Zeit, blieb,
　　　es beim Stein zu versuchen—er
　　　war nicht gastlich, er
　　　fiel nicht ins Wort. Wie
　　　gut wir es hatten:

　　　Körnig,
　　　körnig und faserig. Stengelig,
　　　dicht;
　　　traubig und strahlig; nierig,
　　　plattig und
　　　klumpig; locker, ver-
　　　ästelt—: er, es
　　　fiel nicht ins Wort, es
　　　sprach,
　　　sprach gerne zu trockenen Augen, eh
　　　　　es sie schloß.

　　　Yes.
　　　Cyclones, par-
　　　ticle flurry, there was
　　　time left, time
　　　for an attempt with the stone—it
　　　was hospitable, it
　　　did not interrupt. How
　　　lucky we were:

Grainy,
grainy and stringy. Stalky,
dense;
clumpy and radiate; renal,
flattish and
lumpish; loose, in-
tricate-: he, it
did not interrupt, it
spoke,
willingly spoke to dry eyes and then closed them.

The "stone" stands in opposition to "vegetable," the "dry
eyes" to the "moist" one, the "word" to the "silence." We do
not yet know why the stone has powers not enjoyed by the
organic world—a poetic refutation of scientific knowledge.
But these two stanzas now reveal that the progression of the
text, and of the beings with whose actions this progression
coincides, leads to a renewed attempt to establish a cosmogony at the beginning of the fifth stanza, which begins
the same way ("Cyclones, par-/ticle flurry," VI, 5) as the
opening of VI, 1. This attempt, we are told, forms part of
the text's progression and is one of several attempts that are
not the subject of the poem but the poem itself: "there was
/time left, time/for an attempt with the stone." This time
spent "with the stone" is yet another such attempt, but one
that appears to be succeeding:

[VI, 7] Sprach, sprach.
    War, war.

    Spoke, spoke.
    Was, was.

These two lines return to the dry, laconic language of earlier stanzas, a language that does not merely name its sub-

ject matter but expresses it through the mode of composition; they appear to be reporting and confirming the success of this new tentative cosmogony. This is a reduction of what has just been said, namely, that "he [the stone],[13] it/ did not interrupt, it/*spoke*,/willingly *spoke* to dry eyes and then closed them" and that the stone "*was* hospitable." The doubly double predication ("Spoke, spoke./Was, was") confirms that this "something" (II) that is "audible" (III) and that the "finger" that "gropes up and down, gropes/ around" (IV) attempts to enter, has now reached its goal, and that in fact all the things that have been mentioned thus far in the poem are proving to be one and the same thing. The two lines, themselves doublings of the two verbs (from VI, 5–6), first declare this success by using the verbs "to speak" and "to be," then confirm it by repeating them. At the same time, this two-line stanza, composed solely of the two repeated verbs, declares the identity of language and existence, of poetic text and poetic reality. The successful creation of a world by means of language—which might explain why this new world and its origins are evoked by such a disconcerting flood of words—is taken up again in the two last stanzas of the sixth section.

But first we should note the affinity, perhaps even the identity, of the "stone" that "did not interrupt," that "willingly spoke to dry eyes" (VI, 6), and the persons to whom it is speaking, the ones who, before their "attempt with the stone," with the "eye/the moist one," chose "a/green silence, a sepal" (VI, 3). In opposition to this silence stands the word, spoken not by them, but by the stone. This stone, then, is linked to the "dry eyes," which it speaks to "and then closed," while the "moist" eye (V, 2), the reason for the failure, is linked to the vitality of the vegetable universe, which also includes silence, "a sepal, there was/a thought of vegetation attached to it" (VI, 3)—an opposition like the one between "The stones, white" and the "grassblades" at the beginning of the poem. The darkness of the night stands in contrast to the white of the stones and the light of the word that "came through the night,/wished to shine, wished to shine" (V, 1). At the same time, the word "through" suggests that the light and the darkness are not irremediably opposed, but rather that it is precisely by means of this darkness, by passing through it, that the light comes into being—a lesson in mediation that is repeated in stanza VI, 6.

While all the adjectives in this stanza seem at first to refer to the stone (their gender is indeterminate in the German), and the lines leading up to them make us expect a description of the state implied in "How/lucky we were" "with the stone," some of them do in fact suggest stone (*körnig* ["grainy"], *plattig* ["flattish"], *klumpig* ["lumpish," "in chunks"], *locker* ["loose," "not densely packed"]), while others invoke the vegetable world (*faserig* ["stringy"], *stengelig* ["stalky"], *traubig* ["clumpy," "like a bunch of grapes"], *verästelt* ["intricate," "many-branched"]), and the rest might refer to either stone or plant (*dicht* ["dense"], *strahlig* ["radiate"], *nierig* ["renal," "kidney-shaped"]). This catalogue of unusual adjectives supports the notion of mediation also expressed in the movement from the masculine pronoun ("he" or "it," referring to the stone) to the neuter "it" in "he, it/did not interrupt" (VI, 6). Already at the beginning of the poem, the pairing of "The stones, white" with "grass, written asunder" and "shadows of grassblades" (I, 2) bears witness to this union. These two entities, stone and grass, black-and-white opposites, must join together to produce writing, text. This sheds new light on the opposition between the word that "came through the night" and "wished to shine" (V, 1), on the one hand, and the "ashes" of "Night-

and-night" (V, 2), on the other. We have placed a great deal of emphasis on the caesura in the composition of the fifth section, but the opposition between these two stanzas also serves to pave the way for the mediation that is realized not only in the stanza composed of adjectives (VI, 6), but in the poem as a whole.

> [VI, 8–9] Wir
> > ließen nicht locker, standen
> > inmitten, ein
> > Porenbau, und
> > es kam.
>
> > Kam auf uns zu, kam
> > hindurch, flickte
> > unsichtbar, flickte
> > an der letzten Membran,
> > und
> > die Welt, ein Tausendkristall,
> > schoß an, schoß an.
>
> > We
> > did not let go, we stood
> > in the midst, a
> > porous edifice, and
> > it came.
>
> > Came toward us, came
> > through, stitched
> > invisibly, stitched
> > on the last membrane,
> > and
> > the world, a myriad crystal,
> > shot up, shot up.

While the last line, taking up the diction of VI, 7, contains only a statement and its reiteration, the rest of the stanza appears to be refuting a number of earlier passages; since the poem has been unfolding within its own temporal dimension, one might say it is now bearing witness to a progression that has been completed, an arrival. The world has now been created. The ones once overcome by "sleep" (II) now do not "let go"; the ones between whom lay "something" that prevented them from seeing "through it" have now themselves become "a/porous edifice," through which (*hindurch*) they have been approached ("Came toward us") by something that will join with them to cause the world to "shoot up."

Now that time has been recaptured and reality re-created, now that the word has begun to speak, the adventure of the author/reader subject appears to be over: "and/it came" (VI, 8). What is this recaptured time, this refound reality, this recovered existence? From where does the stone draw its power and the dry eyes their strength, and what is the source of this strange affinity, identity even, between the stone and the living creatures, between the night and those who are traversing it? If these questions were to remain unanswered, they would trap the poem within the hermetic universe of the Symbolist tradition, making it a testimonial to the arbitrariness of poetic creation. This would be a highly inappropriate response to "Engführung," despite Celan's radical rejection of the principle of representation, of Aristotelian mimesis, as is demonstrated in the poem's final three sections.

The "reprise" at the juncture of the sixth and seventh sections is the first and only one in the entire poem to introduce a new word. The repeated expressions have been expanded to announce a new element:

[VII]   Schoß an, schoß an.
                    Dann—

Nächte, entmischt. Kreise,
grün oder blau, rote
Quadrate: die
Welt setzt ihr Innerstes ein
im Spiel mit den neuen
Stunden. —Kreise,
rot oder schwarz, helle
Quadrate, kein
Flugschatten,
kein
Meßtisch, keine
Rauchseele steigt und spielt mit.

          Shot up, shot up.
                 Then—

Nights, unmixed. Circles,
green or blue, red
squares: the
world stakes its innermost
in the game with the new
hours. —Circles,
red or black, bright
squares, no
flight shadow,
no
plane table, no
smoke soul ascends and joins in.

The (re-)creation of the world through the remembrance of the living creatures and the advent of the word—an event recalled by the repeated words (*Schoß an, schoß an*)—is echoed in the introductory *Dann*, which rhymes with the *an* that precedes it. The rhyme accentuates the event that is to occur. The seventh section describes this event, again taking up the "flurry" of the "particle"-words from stanza VI, 6, but replacing the mix of organic and inorganic adjectives with the geometrical elements and colors that make up the "myriad crystal" that, according to the end of the sixth section, is identical to the world that "shot up." But the discourse of this seventh section also differs from that of VI in its use of phrases that introduce or interrupt the sequence of colorful geometrical shapes, allowing the poem, now that the "flurry" has passed, to find its way back to its original language. This language is becoming increasingly resistant to translation, since its dominant mode is essentially based on ambiguity and polysemy, which to an even greater extent now than earlier in the poem involves replacing direct statements with the range of allusions allowed by the various meanings of a single word. What results is a language, by definition untranslatable, in which the words to which the poet has ceded the initiative "illumine one another with reciprocal reflections like a virtual streak of flame upon jewels."[14] For one thing, the word that expresses the mode of action by which the world is being created, *anschiessen* ("to shoot up" in the sense of move or grow quickly), recalls *schiessen* ("to shoot"), which is suggested by the "bullet trap" in section VIII and whose importance will soon become evident.[15]

The state that follows, introduced in the "reprise" before the seventh section by the word "Then," is characterized above all by the nights that are "unmixed." We aren't told what sort of "unmixing" or "demixing" this is. But the placement of this expression immediately after the emphatic "Then" makes it clear (and here we must revert to a musical form of reading) that these "Nights, unmixed" stand in opposition to that other "Night./Night-and-night" (V, 2), which was traversed by the word that "wished to shine" (V, 1). The word has arrived, and the world has been reconstituted, but the nights have by no means been replaced by days, the path of "Engführung" not being one that leads from darkness to light. All that has been attained thus far in the movement of the poem as reconstructed by our reading is that we have been able to progress beyond this *bad* nonbeing, this sleep and this night that are nothing more than sleep, "silence" that is "poison-quenched" (VI, 3), and night that "needs no stars" (I, 3). That this new cosmos of "nights, unmixed" stands in opposition to the one preceding the advent of the word, the "shooting up" of this "world, a myriad crystal" (VI, 9), is confirmed by the second piece of information contained in the stanza: This crystalline world now "stakes its innermost/in the game with the new/hours." The hour that at the beginning of the poem had "no sisters" (I, 3) now has new ones (VII, 1): The forward motion that began with this final hour, the road that, paradoxically, was taken at the moment of the arrival "at home," has led us to a new time. But what characterizes this time, this "unmixing," this crystalline purity, is also the distance from the point of departure that is simultaneously the point of return, the forgetting of those whose memory the poet took upon himself to preserve, a memory that is the source of his poetry's strength. This is suggested in the final lines of the stanza in the negative definitions of the world of "nights, *un*mixed": "no/flight shadow,/no/plane table, no/smoke soul ascends and joins in." This triple negation, whatever the "value" of the thing whose absence is being pointed out, affirms the presence of the void, the "flaw" in this "world, a myriad crystal" (VI, 9) that has just been created. Admittedly it is not stated outright what "flight shadow," what "plane table,"[16] what "smoke soul" are being referred to. This is no doubt an example of what rhetorical theoreticians call *obscuritas*, intentional obscurity, so it cannot be the task of our reading to exhaust the hypotheses that would explain the meaning of these three expressions. Instead, we should note and attempt to characterize this obscurity without losing track of what, both despite and because of this obscurity, is becoming apparent.

This obscurity differs from the sort we saw at the beginning of the poem: "Deported to the/terrain/with the unmistakable trace." There, the definite article presupposes a knowledge that these lines, by their very position at the poem's opening, deny. Here, on the other hand, nothing indicates that the reader ought to know *exactly* what is at issue. Not that we wish to charge the poet with imprecision. Not long before writing "Engführung," Celan described the language of his poetry by saying that in spite of its "necessary ambiguity" (*bei aller unabdingbaren Vielstelligkeit des Ausdrucks*), he was striving for "precision."[17] Thus, we are not betraying the precision of "Engführung" if we resist the temptation to propose a complete explication of what might be meant by "flight shadow," "plane table," and "smoke soul," since such an "explication" would necessarily have recourse to associations that are personal and thus fortuitous, to vague hypotheses. On the contrary—the very respect for precision forces us to limit ourselves to the observation, for example, that the main emphasis in this passage is on negation, absence, with the word *kein(e)* concluding three of the lines and in one case constituting an entire line of its own: "no/flight shadow,/no/plane table, no/smoke soul ascends and joins in." Moreover, the first and the last of these three expressions ("flight shadow" and "smoke soul") describe a motion that enacts a mediation between heaven and earth, while the second ("plane table") is part of the world of man as he makes his home on earth. Which comes down to saying that the "world, a myriad crystal" with its "Nights, unmixed"—even though it "stakes its innermost/in the game with the new/hours"—cannot be the ultimate goal of the path followed by the poem. Something is missing, an element that is perhaps even essential. What characteristics it must have to fulfill the claims implied in the negations ("no/flight shadow,/no/plane table, no/smoke soul ascends and joins in") is something we will learn in the poem's eighth stanza. But our reading is already in a position to note that this crystalline universe of pure forms ("circles," "squares") and bright colors ("Circles,/red or black, bright/squares") is lacking all movement and mediation—there is nothing terrestrial about it, nothing mixed.

Beginning here in the seventh section, our reading can confirm the ambiguity of the expressions *Flugschatten* ("flight shadow") and *Rauchseele* ("smoke soul"), an ambiguity that transcends the level of the "signifier" (more than simple polysemy is at work here). The use Celan makes of German's capacity to create endless new compound words is one of the most significant characteristics of his language. This is not merely a stylistic trait (insofar as there can be such a thing). These composite words allow Celan not only to speak in condensed syntagmas, to "trap" discursive language within isolated words, but to trap it in such a way that the predication attains a level of freedom it would not otherwise have, given the limits of syntactical ambiguity (on which Mallarmé's language famously relies). Because these composite words result from the condensation of syntagmas, it isn't necessary to decide which of the (two or more) parts that make up a word determine the others, and by what means. Thus, *Flugschatten* might signify (or, more precisely: signifies) both "shadow of flight" and "flying shadow," and *Rauchseele* not only "soul composed of smoke," but also "smoke soul" (smoke taken as a soul) or "soul of the smoke." This essential ambiguity, which works on the levels of signified and signifier simultaneously—with the consequence that applying the Saussurian model of the "sign" to an analysis of Celan's language is as inappropriate as it would be for Mallarmé[18]—explains in part why this "world, a myriad crystal," which is composed of geometrical elements, is deficient. Once it has been "unmixed," it no longer contains the differences that constituted its "mixedness" and caused it to engage in mediation through the mixing process. This world is too pure. On the other hand, thanks to what we have been calling the musical composition of the poem, one of the possible significations in each of these two cases (that is: one of the sets of relations that unite the parts of the composite words "flight shadow" and "smoke soul") paves the way for the eighth, climactic section of the poem. Here, too, we see the use of an "enharmonic" of sorts, when the final subject of section VII is repeated unnamed in the transition between VII and VIII, two lines in which only the predicate is reprised.

[VIII, 1]   Steigt und
                                     spielt mit—

        In der Eulenflucht, beim
        versteinerten Aussatz,
        bei
        unsern geflohenen Händen, in
        der jüngsten Verwerfung,
        überm
        Kugelfang an
        der verschütteten Mauer:

                        Ascends and
                                     joins in—

        At owl's flight, near
        the leprous petrifaction,

near
our fugitive hands, in
the most recent casting out,
above
the bullet trap on
the half-buried wall:

The opening of this section is preceded by a predicate deprived of its subject, a predicate taken from section VII, where the subject is "smoke soul." This means—if we "read" the hinge—that this predicate will apply as well to whatever follows in the eighth section, whether the predicate is given a new subject or some other element replaces the subject from section VII. Stanza VIII, 1 appears, at least at first glance, to call for the second sort of construction, since it is composed entirely of adverbial phrases of place and time— in fact, it isn't always possible to distinguish between the two, and this uncertainty creates yet another sort of ambiguity, one that reveals the hidden identity of time and place.

These adverbial phrases make up the entire stanza and thus are not in fact complements, strictly speaking, but themselves predicates. The fact that the predication in this stanza, one of the most significant in the poem, consists entirely of adverbial phrases shows what an important function is assigned to these adverbs in the poem's composition. The adverbs replace and cancel out—in a movement comparable to the rhetorical *correctio*, whose importance for Celan we have already mentioned—the pure, clean, bright elements of the crystalline world that seems to be the culmination of the creative work of the word that "came" and the living creatures who open themselves to it ("We/did not let go, we stood/in the midst, a/porous edifice, and/it came"). At the end of this journey of memory, the "world, a myriad crystal" with its "Nights, unmixed" has given way to something else altogether. Each of the adverbial phrases/ predicates serves not only to realize it, but also to specify it and to relate it to the other sections of the poem. This is what we must now "read":

In der Eulenflucht ("At owl's flight")—here we have a compound noun whose meaning is obsolete, but this does not make it less evocative, since the composite word is necessarily a "motivated" sign. *Eulenflucht*, according to the Grimms' dictionary, refers to dusk, the hour when owls take flight.[19] A different hour, a different light, are thus introduced into the universe of the poem by this first piece of information. This isn't the night that "needs no stars" (I, 3), the night of those who "did not see through it" once sleep had come over them (II, 2), but it is also not the "unmixed" night of the world that "stakes its innermost/in the game with the new/hours" (VII), this world of "bright/squares." It is an hour of transition, of mediation, of the passage between day and night. But it is also the hour of escape, *Flucht* ("flight") being the noun that corresponds not only to *fliegen* ("to fly") but also to *fliehen* ("to flee"). The third adjectival phrase supports this second sense:

"Near/our fugitive hands"—we have already spoken at length of the role played in the poem by the finger ("a finger/gropes up and down, gropes/around," IV) and the hand ("How/did we touch/one another—touch with/ these/hands?" VI, 2). This role is not simply thematic (if there is such a thing); it would also be possible to call it "rhetorical" if it did not represent precisely a having gone beyond the rhetorical figure synecdoche. "Finger" as it is used here does not replace the word that stands for the thing it forms part of "in reality"; it is most certainly "a finger" that is feeling the strange, uneven surface of this traumatic past. And the place described in the eighth section is no longer the place of those who have taken flight, but of "our fugitive hands"—the hands referred to in the question of VI, 2 ("How/did we touch/one another"), whose touch did not bring about the resurrection of the past in memory; on the contrary: "We/put a silence upon it,/ . . . a/green/silence, a sepal, there was /a thought of vegetation attached to it" (VI, 3). The place of the hands that have fled stands in opposition to that nonplace: "the world, a myriad crystal" (VI, 9), a pure, bright world, a new world, but one whose creation is increasingly proving insufficient, although it partakes in this event that is constituted by and constitutes the poem, and since the poem is a progression, this means precisely that the creation of this world is something that must be gotten beyond. This creation is also insufficient for the reason that it has been reduced to the crystalline, inorganic, pure—an ensemble of geometrical shapes, circles, and squares of colors that are themselves pure: "Circles,/green or blue, red/squares" (VII)—a pure world, free of mixing, that is, of mediation, the mediation between stone and plant that announces, as we have seen, the sequence of adjectives ("Grainy,/grainy and stringy. Stalky,/dense"; VI, 6) as well as the passage from "he" to "it" ("he, it/did not interrupt," VI, 6). This same mediation characterizes the passage described in the eighth section:

Beim/versteinerten Aussatz ("near/the leprous petrifaction")—the word *Aussatz* is ambiguous, since it signifies more than just "leprosy."[20] The word is derived from *aussetzen* ("to cast out," "to expose"), the action to which persons infected with this illness were subjected. Although *Aussatz*, at least today, no longer signifies anything other than the disease leprosy, the German word in this context (in which the words "illumine one another with reciprocal reflections," to cite Mallarmé's phrase once more), evokes something else as well. To evoke something in poetry means to signify, or, more precisely, to realize something. What is this "exposure"? Another line from this same stanza, itself an adjectival phrase, provides the answer:

In/der jüngsten Verwerfung ("in/the most recent casting out")[21]—this term cannot signify anything other than the fate to which millions of Jews were subjected during the Nazi era, among them the parents of the poet, the last of the reprobations that have been inflicted on the people of Israel since the beginning of their history. The place described and dated by the various adjectival phrases in this stanza is beyond all doubt that of the "final solution," the *Endlösung*: the death camp. The Jews, rejected so many times in the course of their long history by the communities in which they lived, accused of being carriers of the plague (*Aussätzige*), have now been cast out, exposed (*ausgesetzt*), or, to use the term that is, for good reason, the first word of the poem: "deported."

Überm/Kugelfang an/der verschütteten Mauer ("above/the bullet trap on/the half-buried wall")—these are the last two pieces of information that define this place, which is laden down with a past that is not and will never be truly past. The "bullet trap" is attached to the "half-buried wall"— *verschüttet* ("buried in rubble"), perhaps because the present in this section seems to refer to a later epoch. This "bullet trap" marks the upper boundary of this place of extermination. The action in the eighth section of the poem takes place "above/the bullet trap on/the half-buried wall." The other adjectival phrases—introduced not by the preposition "above," but by "in" and "near," which appear twice each— refer to a place and a time on this side of the boundary line, while the expression introduced by "above" points to something that crosses this boundary the moment it arrives. The colon at the end of the first stanza ("on/the half-buried wall:") indicates that we are about to learn what is there.

> [VIII, 2] sichtbar, aufs
>   neue: die
>   Rillen, die
>
>   visible, once
>   more: the
>   grooves, the

What arrives and crosses the boundaries that mark out this site of rejection, exposure, and death is an appearance, an epiphany. Not of a god, but of the *Rillen* ("grooves")— the *Spuren*, or traces, to return to the beginning of the poem. What are these "grooves"? "Engführung," which is not the poem of a progression, an advent, but is itself this advent, is itself self-realizing knowledge, knowledge of the nature of this advent, has now reached a point where these questions can no longer go unanswered, or, more precisely: where the advent has made answers possible. For this reason, having placed the words "the/grooves" after the colon announcing that we are about to learn what has become "visible, once/more" in this space "above," the poet continues: "the/grooves, the." Then, after a brief but highly expressive interval between the definite article and the noun it governs, an interval that marks not just the end of a line, but the end of a stanza:

> [VIII, 3] Chöre, damals, die
>   Psalmen. Ho, ho-
>   sianna.
>
>   choruses, once, the
>   psalms. Ho, ho-
>   sanna.

It is known that the deported Jews often would begin to pray and sing psalms when faced with execution. *Hosianna* in Hebrew means "save, I beg you" or "save now." This prayer goes beyond the upper boundary defined by the "bullet trap" and provides a means for those who recite it to go beyond the domain of their sufferings; thus, the prayer is, in a sense, itself a "bullet trap." Their salvation is the *word*, language. Of course, the poet says nothing of the sort. All he speaks of is the lesson to be drawn from the conduct of the deported Jews marching to their deaths. The poem evokes facts that belong to historical reality, and this evocation in turn becomes the poem's end (in both senses) so as to make of it a lesson.

[VIII, 4–5]   Also
stehen noch Tempel. Ein
Stern
hat wohl noch Licht.
Nichts,
nichts ist verloren.

Ho-
sianna.

So
there are temples yet. A
star
may yet have light.
Nothing,
nothing is lost.

Ho-
sanna.

The term *Also* ("So," "Thus") at the beginning of the fourth stanza indicates there is a lesson here, a consequence to be drawn. If the temples are still real and still stand, it is because prayers were spoken (in the place where no temples stood), and, to an even greater extent, because of these words: "The // choruses" "the/psalms" of an earlier era are becoming "visible, once/more," in the form of the "grooves" forever engraved in the memory of humankind by those who sang them "in/the most recent casting out." If there is memory—*Gedächtnis, Eingedenken*—it is thanks to the traces that have been left behind by the victims to whom memory is now returning. Thanks to the word. But what constitutes this memory and makes it not just an obligation, but a *poetic* obligation and necessity, is that it bears witness to the creative power of the word, that is, to the verbal origins of reality—at least of the reality that matters. And so the evocation of the death camps is not only the end of Celan's poetry, but its precondition. "Engführung" is in a quite precise sense a refutation of Theodor W. Adorno's now all-too famous thesis: "After Auschwitz, one can no longer write poetry."[22] Adorno, who for years had wanted to write a long essay on Celan, whom he considered the most important postwar writer besides Beckett, understood perfectly well that his thesis was open to misunderstanding, and perhaps even false.[23] After Auschwitz, one can no longer write poetry, except with respect to Auschwitz. Nowhere did Celan demonstrate more clearly or convincingly than in "Engführung" how well-founded the secret credo of his work was, its essentially nonconfessional, impersonal character. The creating word is not the mysterious word of which we read in the first stanza of section V that it "came,/came through the night,/wished to shine, wished to shine." It is the one offered up by the deported at the moment of their death, the word whose "grooves" become "visible" again at the end of the poem. Now we are in a position to understand the radical opposition of the fifth section's two stanzas. The first, consecrated to the word that comes to shine, clashes with the second: "Ashes./Ashes, ashes./Night./Night-and-night.— Go/to the eye, the moist one." So the reality of the ashes, the reality of the death camps and their crematoria, is only seemingly an obstacle to the advent of the word, to the re-creation of the world by means of language, since "the world, a myriad crystal," which "shot up" (VI, 9) and which stands in opposition to that other world whose creation has been stifled by repression, by the "silence . . . /poison-quenched, huge,/a/green/silence, a sepal" that was imposed on it (VI, 3), is no longer the universe that creates, the universe that *is* "Engführung": "no/flight shadow,/no/plane table, no/smoke soul ascends and joins in" (VII). And it is not this universe precisely because there are two worlds here standing opposed to one another, because there is opposition—between word and silence, stone and plant, dry eyes and the moist one. But the song ("the // choruses, once, the/psalms"), like the reality ("So/there are temples yet") and the radiance ("A/star/may yet have light"), comes into being only once this opposition has been abolished, comes about through the "leprous petrifaction," through going beyond the nothingness that is rejection (the *Verwerfung*): "Nothing,/nothing is lost" (VIII, 4).

Yet making such a statement without restriction of any sort, without acknowledging its fragility, the cracks in it and the painful doubt, would come down to distorting the poem. Several crucial facts have not yet been pointed out. For example, the use of line breaks, the fractured words: "Ho, ho-/sanna" (VIII, 3), "Nothing,/nothing is lost" (VIII, 4), "Ho-/sanna" (VIII, 5). Whoever it is who is speaking here, be it the poet or those whose memory he is evoking, is having difficulty speaking. The "Hosanna" doesn't come out easily. After the first syllable, its word, its

prayer, is interrupted. This attempt at addressing God begins as a cry, profane, even vulgar: "Ho, ho—." Similarly,
the star only "*may* yet have light." And the break between
the next two lines ("Nothing,/nothing is lost"), once
"read," tells us it is no longer even certain, at least not for
the moment, that nothing has been lost. The first thing we
read here is the word "Nothing." It doesn't mean that *nothing* has been lost, it isn't the first word of a sentence that will
go on to say this. "Nothing" means "nothing." Only after
having *said*, or rather *posited* the word "nothing," perhaps,
is it possible for the poet to go on to assure us that "nothing is lost." There can be existence here only when it transforms itself into the memory, the "trace," of nonexistence.
And so even though the word "may" no longer figures in
the next sentence ("Nothing,/nothing is lost"), both the
fractured word and the doubt return in the stanza that follows: "Ho-/sanna" (VIII, 5).

At the end of the eighth section, the conclusion of the
poem, the function of this section within the poem as a
whole remains to be investigated.

Reading the musical element at the opening of this section: "Ascends and/joins in—" demonstrates how the
eighth section is connected to the seventh—the jointure itself shows this. As we have said, it is formed from the predicate of the preceding sentence, whose last subject ("smoke
soul") is suppressed. Reading the eighth section makes the
reason for this suppression clear, but it is also apparent that
the subject continues to assert its presence through the
predicate. Reading the section in which the expression appears, it isn't yet possible to know what is meant by the
"smoke soul"; only in the eighth section is this revealed,
since the place of the "bullet trap" is also that of the crematoria whose "ashes" have been evoked in a previous section

(V, 2). This is not the only link between the negations of the seventh section and the affirmations of the eighth; "no/ flight shadow" is taken up again in the "owl's flight," the hour when day gives way to night, earth to sky. This "mixed" hour, which stands in opposition to the "nights, unmixed" (VII, 1) of a too-pure world, one lacking both mediation and communication, where there is "no/flight shadow,/no/plane table," where "no/smoke soul ascends and joins in"—this hour of dusk is evoked one last time, at the end of the eighth section, before the poem returns, in parentheses, to the lines with which it began.

> [VIII, 6] In der Eulenflucht, hier,
> die Gespräche, taggrau,
> der Grundwasserspuren.
>
> At owl's flight, here,
> the conversations, day-gray,
> of the groundwater traces.

The "groundwater traces" speak just as "the grooves" speak "above/the bullet trap." The heights correspond to the depths, the "light" of "A/star" (VIII, 5) to the "day-gray" of the earth. But what does it mean to correspond? If "Engführung" is writing itself as progression, if reading it consists of retracing (rather than reproducing) this progression, then the "groundwater traces" do not *correspond* to the celestial "grooves" of the prayer, they *follow* them. They follow them in three different senses of the word: (1) The poem replaces the "grooves"—which are higher up—with the "groundwater traces"; (2) "the conversations . . . of the groundwater traces" are today what the "grooves, the // choruses, once, the/psalms" once were; (3) the "groundwater traces" are speaking at the same hour—"At owl's flight"

(VIII, 1 and VIII, 6)—as the "grooves . . . // once": these "traces" today are succeeding those of the "grooves" of former times, "visible, once/more" (VIII, 2). "The conversations, day-gray,/of the groundwater traces" derive from the "choruses," the prayers from the time of the "most recent casting out." The way one remembers them determines who one is and what one does today.

But is it really clear that these "groundwater traces"— even if we read of their "conversations," the exchange of words, as opposed to the "spoke of/words" in the second section—are standing in, "here" (VIII, 6), for something that has been sought after since the beginning of the poem? What suggests this is the repetition of the poem's first lines in parentheses at the end, following the stanza we have just been analyzing.

[IX, 1–2]   (——taggrau,
                        der
                                Grundwasserspuren—
            Verbracht
            ins Gelände
            mit
            der untrüglichen
            Spur:
            Gras.
            Gras,
            auseinandergeschrieben.)

                    (——day-gray,
                            of
                                the groundwater traces—
            Deported to the
            terrain
            with

> the unmistakable
> trace:
>
> grass.
> Grass,
> written asunder.)

Let no one claim the poem is describing a circle and returning to its point of departure. The parentheses alone
should be enough to show how inexact such an interpretation is. They make us pronounce these lines sotto voce,
slowed by the shifts in the line breaks. These lines are being
recalled only to shed light on those that precede them: "the
conversations, day-gray,/of the groundwater traces." And so
the function of the repetition of the opening lines at the
conclusion of "Engführung" corresponds to the function of
the "reprises" in the jointures between sections. Here, the
repetition is forging a link between "the conversations . . . /
of the groundwater *traces*" and the "terrain/with the unmistakable *trace*." But the "unmistakable trace" and the
"groundwater traces" are one and the same thing: language,
word.

The reader who was "Deported to the/terrain/with the
unmistakable trace" (I, 1) was neither able nor supposed to
know what this "unmistakable trace" was. Now, having
reached the end of the progression that was our reading, a
reading of something that is itself a progression, he understands. And this is why no explanation is being offered him.
Once again, the reader has the opportunity to ignore the
laws of musical composition and ask: What is the meaning
of "the conversations, day-gray,/of the groundwater traces"?
And again, it is not by studying other passages in Celan's
work where such expressions appear that the answer will be
found (though readers are encouraged to engage in such

study by the existence of a concordance that was published several years ago). While at the beginning of the poem the reader was forced to come to terms with the fact that he was apparently not yet supposed to know what was being spoken of, it is now assumed that he already does know what is being referred to, that the "groundwater traces" are "the/ grooves, the // choruses, once, the/psalms," but at the same time also the "unmistakable trace" that characterizes this "terrain" in which he has been moving since he began to read, without knowing where he was. The poem's opening is repeated for the purpose of his knowing. The "conversations . . . /of the groundwater traces" and their communication by means of the word "replace," at the end of the poem, the noncommunication of the ones who both were and were not lying there, because "Something/lay between them" (II, 1). Both the isolation that caused them to speak "of words" of which "None/awoke" (II, 2) and the "silence . . . /poison-quenched" that they "put . . . upon it" (VI, 3) have been overcome.

The "groundwater"—in contrast both to this world of "silence" and repression and to the nonworld of what is "unmixed," the "world, a myriad crystal"—is the mediation and thus the negation of the two opposed elements, the negation of the negation. Like the "leprous petrifaction" (VIII, 1). If the "groundwater traces" speak, if there is communication ("conversations"), it is because these traces are language, water beneath the earth, water within the earth (stone), "trace" of one thing within another, just as the "shadows of grassblades," uniting "The stones, white" and the "grass," creates writing: "Grass, written asunder" (I, 2). An "underneath," a ground (*Grund-wasserspuren*): the condition of possibility for the textual reality of "Engführung," the human condition today, "At owl's flight, here" (VIII, 6), the condition of a humanity that, who knows how, survived Auschwitz and continues to survive it, who knows how.

One final remark: That the poem bears the title "Engführung" can be explained by the analogy between the part of a fugue known by this name and the specific composition of Celan's text. We have already spoken of this at great length. But this is not—could never be—more than just a partial explanation. The German word *Engführung* is a technical term. But as a "motivated sign" (being a word made up of parts), it is also a designation that is not only self-explanatory, but contributes to the explication of the poem whose title it is (while at the same time being explained by it). In other words, it is also a *name. Engführung,* the noun associated with the syntagma *eng führen* ("to lead while drawing more tightly together"), is thus not only linked to the principle of musical composition evoked by the form of composition the poet has chosen. The term does not designate merely the arrangement into "sections" that are like "voices," the "voices" brought together in the jointures between sections by the use of "reprises." The title "Engführung" also indicates that the poem is a progression, that the text is laying open a path for the reader. This progression of the reader and of the text he is reading comes about through the linking of sections drawn together by the "reprises." It comes about by means of a path that traverses the memory of the death camps. This commemoration becomes the basis for the poet's "conversations."

"Engführung," stretto, being led through the strait—does this title, which is a name, designate the *strict* manner in which the poet leads the poem? Or the road his reading forces the reader to follow, to retrace? Or even the commemoration of the straits of the "most recent casting out"? He who has learned to "read" Celan's writing knows it isn't a matter of selecting one of several meanings, but of understanding that they do not *differ*, but coincide. Ambiguity, which has become a means of knowledge, shows us the unity of what only appeared to be difference. This ambiguity serves the cause of precision.

§ 3 Eden

When Celan died, he left behind the completed manuscript of *Schneepart*, a collection of poems dating from the last years of his life. In the book, one finds these lines:

> Du liegst im großen Gelausche,
> umbuscht, umflockt.
>
> Geh du zur Spree, geh zur Havel,
> geh zu den Fleischerhaken,
> zu den roten Äppelstaken
> aus Schweden—
>
> Es kommt der Tisch mit den Gaben,
> er biegt um ein Eden—
>
> Der Mann ward zum Sieb, die Frau
> mußte schwimmen, die Sau,
> für sich, für keinen, für jeden—
>
> Der Landwehrkanal wird nicht rauschen.
> Nichts
>   stockt.[1]

> You lie amid a great listening,
> enhedged, enflaked.

Go to the Spree, to the Havel,
to the butchers' hooks,
the red apple stakes
from Sweden—

Now comes the gift-laden table,
it turns around an Eden—

The man became a sieve, the woman,
the sow, had to swim,
for herself, for no one, for everyone—

The Landwehr Canal will not murmur.
Nothing
        stops.

One of the few poems in *Schneepart* to be published during Celan's lifetime (in *Hommage für Peter Huchel, zum 3.
April 1968*),[2] this work was originally labeled "Berlin, December 22/23, 1967." The reader need not know where the
poem was written to understand it, because the text itself
makes clear references to Berlin. The dates of composition
are more significant: The poem was written the night of
December 22—it is a night poem, a pre-Christmas poem.
The text alludes to both these things: *Du liegst* ("You lie," 1)
suggests the hour, and *der Tisch mit den Gaben* ("the gift-
laden table," 7) the imminent feast. Celan later removed the
references to city and date, which appear neither in
Schneepart nor in the earlier volume, *Ausgewählte Gedichte*,
where the poem was also printed.[3] It was Celan's usual practice to date his poems in manuscript, but not in their final
published form, so it isn't the absence of this information in
Schneepart that is surprising, but rather its presence in the
Huchel *Festschrift*. One possible explanation is that the
poem, like two others in the volume that were also dated
and labeled "Frankfurt am Main/Berlin" and "Berlin," was

to be understood as a tribute to Huchel, who was then living on the outskirts of Berlin. So the later absence of date and place, which makes the poem less immediately accessible ("Du liegst" becomes ambiguous, and the *roten Äppelstaken/aus Schweden* ["the red apple stakes/from Sweden"] lose the date that would supply their context), should not necessarily be read as an attempt to obscure the traces that might lead us back to the circumstances of the poem's genesis. But, seen objectively, this *is* the effect of the deletion. And the fact that the first printed version of the poem (in *Hommage für Peter Huchel*) omits its original title suggests that this effect was intentional. Celan had kept the title "Wintergedicht" (Winter poem) when he copied out the poem for friends—including the copy (the original?) he sent a friend on December 29, 1967, the day of his departure from Berlin—but this time, the title was crossed out.[4] Even this might be explained by Celan's ever more consistent rejection, in his later work, of the institution of the titled poem.[5] At the same time, a knowledge of the real-life referent, Celan's experiences in Berlin around Christmas 1967 that found their way into the poem, cannot itself constitute an interpretation. Rather, such knowledge gives us access to the history of the poem's genesis, in which almost every passage refers to a documented event and illumines the path that led from the actual experiences to their transformation in the poem. For this reader, who was fortunate enough to spend these days in Celan's company, the poem appears to exist in the charged space between the half-random assortment of images and events marking Celan's stay in Berlin and the artful constellation that is the poem. The intention of this essay, then, is not to reduce the poem to the dates and facts that produced these fourteen lines, but rather to attempt to retrace the process of this crystallization.

Celan arrived in Berlin on December 16, 1967. He had passed through the city on his way to France in 1938,[6] but otherwise this was his first (and only) visit here. The immediate occasion was a reading that Walter Höllerer had arranged in the Studio of the Akademie der Künste (Academy of the Arts). The following day, Celan gave a reading of poems from *Atemwende* (Breath turn), which had just appeared, before a small group of students and professors at the Department of Comparative Literature at the Freie Universität Berlin. Aside from a television recording session conducted by Ernst Schnabel (December 27), Celan had no other obligations during his stay in Berlin. He visited friends, let them show him around the snow-covered city, and registered the ubiquitous manifestations of Christmas cheer with the puzzled receptiveness of one who belongs to a people that does not know this holiday and who has lived for years in a land that does not greet it with "cheer"—but also of one who is (perhaps) still familiar with it from his distant childhood, the far-off land of his birth.

Celan was housed in the Akademie der Künste, a modern building in the Hansa district where the large windows of his room—which filled one entire wall—gave onto part of the Tiergarten park that was planted with bushes. Here, one night, he wrote the lines:

> Du liegst im großen Gelausche,
> umbuscht, umflockt.

A friend accompanied him to Plötzensee to see the room where the July 20 conspirators had been executed.[7] He also showed Celan the Christmas market set up at the base of the radio tower, featuring displays of goods from various countries. At one of the stands, the Swedish one, Celan saw an Advent wreath made of red-painted wood that held apples and candles. These two elements were combined in the poem's second stanza:

> Geh du zur Spree, geh zur Havel,
> geh zu den Fleischerhaken,
> zu den roten Äppelstaken
> aus Schweden—

On one of his first evenings in Berlin, Celan asked me for a book, saying he had nothing to read with him. I gave him a volume that had recently appeared, *Der Mord an Rosa Luxemburg und Karl Liebknecht: Dokumentation eines politischen Verbrechens.*[8] On one of our drives from my apartment to the Akademie der Künste, I showed him the Eden apartment building, which had been constructed on the site of the old Eden Hotel, where in January 1919, when it was serving as headquarters for the Garde-Kavallerie-Schützen-Division (Division of Cavalry and Riflemen), Rosa Luxemburg and Karl Liebknecht spent the last hours of their lives. Next to the Eden stands the Europa-Center, whose shops were decorated for the upcoming festivities. From the Kurfürstendamm, one turns onto Budapester Strasse, which leads to the Tiergarten and the Landwehr Canal. As we drove, we spoke of what contempt it showed for the memory of the two people who had been murdered here that the name "Eden" had been retained for these luxury apartments. This drive may have occasioned the third stanza:

> Es kommt der Tisch mit den Gaben,
> er biegt um ein Eden—

Although the names Rosa Luxemburg and Karl Liebknecht do not appear in the stanza that follows, which includes phrases taken from court protocols reproduced in the volume I'd lent Celan, they are its subject. Walter Alker testified on the witness stand that, when he asked whether Dr. Liebknecht was really already dead, he was told that "Liebknecht was shot full of holes like a sieve."[9] And one of the murderers, a soldier named Runge, reported hearing someone say of Rosa Luxemburg, "The old sow is already swimming."[10] The poem contains the lines:

> Der Mann ward zum Sieb, die Frau
> mußte schwimmen, die Sau,
> [...]

The penultimate line names the Landwehr Canal, into which Rosa Luxemburg's murderers threw her body; during the night of December 20, 1967, Celan followed this canal on his way to visit the ruins of the train station Anhalter Bahnhof,[11] whose façade had been left to stand, a sort of phantom.

This biographical report (others could no doubt make similar remarks apropos of other Celan poems), is not intended as the justification for a reading of the poem "Du liegst im großen Gelausche." Rather, we might ask whether such information can serve to support any reading at all. To what extent does understanding the poem depend on a knowledge of the biographical/historical framework? Or, in more general terms, to what extent is the poem determined by things external to it, and this determination from without invalidated by the poem's own internal logic? Obviously Celan's poem would never have been written—at least not in this form—had it not been for the experiences of his stay in Berlin, which were determined more by his friends and by chance than by the poet himself. Without the drive to the Havel, to the Landwehr Canal, past the Eden, without the visit to the Christmas market, the execution chamber at

Plötzensee, without Celan's having read the Luxemburg/
Liebknecht documentation, the poem would have been impossible. Yet Celan also saw, read, and experienced many
other things during the same few days that left no traces in
the poem. But the poem's determination by everyday coincidence is already limited—indeed precluded—by the
process of selection, which, no less than these more or less
chance occurrences themselves, was a necessary precondition for the poem, part of its genesis. We might ask whether
the determination from without, the real-life referent, is not
balanced out by the poem's self-determination: the interdependence of its various elements, by means of which even
the real events referred to are transformed.

The poem's texture lies in a twofold interweaving of motifs: The motif of the murder of Rosa Luxemburg and Karl
Liebknecht is first linked to that of the execution of the July
20 conspirators (ll. 9–12, 4), then this double motif is interwoven with Christmas imagery (ll. 5–7). While the first
linkage is obviously justified, the second seems fairly scan-
dalous. The first can be traced back to an association with
specific biographical referents (reading the Hannovers'
book, visiting the execution chamber with the "butchers'
hooks"), but the same association might have been made
without the biographical information. On the other hand,
faced with the linkage of murder and execution to Christmas gifts (cf. l. 7), the juxtaposition of "butchers' hooks"
and "apple stakes," one might be tempted to seek interpre-
tational refuge in the record of Celan's actual experiences to
explain this disturbing conjunction. Yet there could be no
greater betrayal of the poem and its author. While this juxtaposition was clearly motivated by the fact that Celan's visit
to Berlin coincided with the Christmas season, the link between the two motifs had to transcend its empirical prem-

ises and find its own justification to make the poem a
poem. Indeed, these empirical premises no doubt became
relevant to the poem's genesis only through an impulse determined not by the actual events of Celan's visit, but by a
reality that cannot be reduced to subjective happenstance.
The lines at the center of the poem point to the secret basis
for the linkage of murder and Christmas festivity:

> Es kommt der Tisch mit den Gaben,
> er biegt um ein Eden—

These two lines, more than any others in the poem, are
characterized by an extreme ambiguity that establishes itself
in their last word, *Eden*. "Eden" signifies not only paradise,
a garden of pleasures, but also the place named for it where
Rosa Luxemburg and Karl Liebknecht spent the final hours
preceding their murder. Anyone who supposes it was *as*
chance, *as* coincidence that this ambiguity—produced by
the chance fact that the hotel bore this name and the division staff of the Garde-Kavallerie-Schützen was quartered
there—became the focal point of the intersection of mur-
der/execution and Christmas motifs is an utter stranger to
the sort of gaze through which Celan observed the contradictions of this world. For Celan, these contradictions were
not contradictory. He was well acquainted with the experience of discovering that milk is black and blackness milk,[12]
that the moral world is neither divided up into good and
evil nor consists of fluctuations between the two, but rather
that good is also evil and that evil, in one way or another,
has some element of good. Anyone who wants to offer a
preconceived explanation for this dialectic will be as far removed from a serious understanding of Celan's life and poetry as he would be if he were to close his eyes to this dialectic altogether. To say that beneath Celan's gaze even the

brightest things took on a somber aspect and that his poetry found light even in darkness is true enough, but it is a simplification and thus also wrong. The conjoining of paradise and purgatory in the word "Eden," the indifference of history and human beings that let the place where Rosa Luxemburg and Karl Liebknecht spent their final hours be named for that paradisiacal pleasure garden and let the luxury apartment building erected on the same site be named for the hotel turned purgatory—this impassivity can only have confirmed Celan's basic experience of an *in-difference*. This is why he was struck by the indifference here and made it the core of his poem.

It is against this background we should read those lines in which the murder and Christmas motifs unite so disturbingly that one might be tempted to invoke the biographical details mentioned above to explain away their conjunction. I am speaking of the lines:

> geh zu den Fleischerhaken,
> zu den roten Äppelstaken
> aus Schweden—

This linkage owes its existence neither to the mere coincidence of two visits Celan made during his stay in Berlin (Plötzensee and Christmas market) nor solely to the basic disposition of his way of seeing that has just been described. If the first is a coincidental, external precondition that made possible the poem's concretization in words, the second is an essential, immanent one that can justify this concretization (the link of "butchers' hooks" and "apple stakes"), but not produce it. The poem as a tissue of words, poised in the charged space of *signifié* and *signifiant*, of sense and sound, and marked by the changing relations between the two, gives concrete form to the association of

thoughts, not discursively, in a fixed sequence of statements, but in the sum of interactions provided for by the
linguistic material—or, in Roman Jakobson's terminology,
not metonymically, but metaphorically.[13] The phonetic correspondence between the words' final syllables (*-aken*) is
only the external manifestation of this equivalence, for the
rhyme also confirms that the *roten Äppelstaken/aus Sweden*,
an emblem of Advent cheer, and the *Fleischerhaken* from
Plötzensee are not unrelated. This relation is revealed
through language, in part by the fact that *Staken* derives
from *stechen* ("to stab" or "poke") and can also mean "pole"
or "pillory."[14] The link is further justified by the threefold
meaning of the adjective of color assigned to the *Äppel-
staken*: they are "red" in the sense of "red-painted" (joining
green, silver, and gold to form the Christmas palette). But
red is also the color of blood, the color that the *Fleischerhaken* and *Staken* become after executions, and red is the
color of the flag for which Rosa Luxemburg and Karl Liebknecht gave their lives.

. . .

Appendix A
Notes on "Eden"

Handwritten notes
(on one page):

1) *Schweden—Eden—jeden*

   Schweden at the beginning is just an explanatory modifier
   (*Äppel-*).

   Setting up Eden.

2) *it turns around an Eden*

   the past is standing in the way of the upcoming celebration

3) The final stanza a return to the beginning (*Gelausche/
   rauschen*; *-flockt/stockt*); the future tense corresponding
   to the imperative (*Geh . . .*).

(on one page):

Eden, the ambiguous, bitter word core of the poem, is embedded in the rhyme sequence *Schweden—Eden—jeden*.
Embedded all the more as each of the two other words contains it.

(on a slip of paper):

> The poem stops short because nothing is stopping.
> The fact that nothing stops makes the poem stop short.

In addition to the fair copy of the existing manuscript, the first typewritten version (eight typed pages containing handwritten corrections) also survives. The final copy, which bears no title, was based on this corrected draft and differs from it only in a small number of minor (stylistic) revisions. The title "Eden" comes from the corrected typescript (as well as the table of contents in a notebook entry).

There also exists a photocopy of the partially corrected first draft bearing the title "Eden Berlin."

At the end of the penultimate section of the essay (after the line "the interdependence of its various elements, by means of which even the real events referred to are transformed"), the typescript contains the following sentences, which Szondi later cut during the revision process: "Since in the following this question [the autonomy versus the contingency of the poem—SB] is to be investigated, or rather: taking as a starting point the working hypothesis that this autonomy of the poem exists and is a worthy object of inquiry, the biographical approach discussed above will be left out of account. If interpretation and structural analysis are often colored by the dilemma of lacking biographical/historical data, which positivism so loved, they can here be put to the test *en connaissance de cause* by a deliberate exclusion of these data motivated by methodological considerations. I will have recourse to them only to confirm that the analysis has not in fact secretly used them as a source of contraband material. At the same time, knowledge of this data, which was presented to the reader before the interpretation, will serve to verify the working hypothesis according to which the poem's determination by the background of real events has had to defer to an autonomy inherent in the immanent logic of the poem."

In the last paragraph, the sentence "The phonetic correspondence between the words' final syllables (-*aken*) is only the external manifestation of this equivalence" was originally followed by: "Rhyme for Celan is not, as for Karl Kraus, *das Ufer, wo sie landen/sind zwei Gedanken einverstanden* ("the shore where they land/are two thoughts in accord").[1]

Appendix B
Notes on "Es war Erde in ihnen"

While only two pages of notes on the poem "Blume" were found among Peter Szondi's papers, we have enough information about the second of his unwritten essays on Celan to identify at least the approach that would have been used in it. The poem "Es war Erde in ihnen" (There was earth inside them) was considered at length in Szondi's seminar on the linguistic analysis of poetry held at the Freie Universität Berlin during the summer semester of 1970. At the beginning of the term, Szondi introduced the method of linguistic analysis using the article by Roman Jakobson and Claude Lévi-Strauss on Baudelaire's poem "Les chats";[1] he supplemented this study with various other analytic works by Jakobson, as well as a number of essays critical of the approach. In the second half of the seminar, the method of linguistic analysis was applied to texts that had been selected by the students. Celan's poem was discussed during the June 25 and July 2 sessions. After a student had presented his analysis for discussion by the group, Szondi offered his own interpretation of the poem, which was meant both to correct and to go beyond the student's work.

We can reconstruct certain main points of Szondi's interpretation on the basis of his annotations in the margins of the student's paper, as well as the—unfortunately rather skimpy—notes taken by several participants. The form this interpretation takes is limited by the scope of the exercise, and so it isn't possible to say what other sorts of analysis the projected essay would have contained, but the principles of linguistic analysis are reflected in other of Szondi's essays as well, and his inclusion of this particular poem in his seminar indicates that he considered it appropriate for analysis of this sort.

Es war Erde in ihnen, und
sie gruben.

Sie gruben und gruben, so ging
ihr Tag dahin, ihre Nacht. Und sie lobten nicht Gott,
der, so hörten sie, alles dies wollte,
der, so hörten sie, alles dies wußte.

Sie gruben und hörten nichts mehr;
sie wurden nicht weise, erfanden kein Lied,
erdachten sich keinerlei Sprache.
Sie gruben.

Es kam eine Stille, es kam auch ein Sturm,
es kamen die Meere alle.
Ich grabe, du gräbst, und es gräbt auch der Wurm,
und das Singende dort sagt: Sie graben.

O einer, o keiner, o niemand, o du:
Wohin gings, das nirgendhin ging?
O du gräbst und ich grab, und ich grab mich dir zu,
und am Finger erwacht uns der Ring.

There was earth inside them, and
they dug.

They dug and they dug, so their day
went by for them, their night. And they did not
    praise God,
who, so they heard, wanted all this,
who, so they heard, knew all this.

They dug and heard nothing more;
they did not grow wise, invented no song,
thought up for themselves no language.
They dug.

There came a stillness, and there came a storm,
and all the oceans came.
I dig, you dig, and the worm digs too,
and that singing out there says: They dig.

O one, o none, o no one, o you:
Where did the way lead when it led nowhere?
O you dig and I dig, and I dig towards you,
and on our finger the ring awakes.[2]

2.

In the paper presented for discussion, Szondi's student begins by analyzing the poem's language, noting for instance
the absence of adjectives, the relatively large number of lexical and empty verbs, and especially of pronominal forms,
but also the fact that the poem contains no compound
words (which prompts Szondi's comment that it "differs in
this respect from most of Celan's poems"). The student's ex-
amination of the syntactical structure resulted in the observation that the sentences are regularly distributed among the
five stanzas (nine sentences: one for the first two lines, and
eight, i.e., two each, for the four quatrains). In terms of the
composition, he notes that the end of each of the sentences
coincides with the end of a line (to which Szondi adds the
important observation that within the stanzas, only in those

that rhyme does the first sentence coincide with the first half of the stanza). The distribution of the individual syntagmatic and lexical elements within each of the stanzas and their phonetic relationships receive similar analysis. These investigations reveal that the caesura in the middle of the penultimate stanza (between lines 12 and 13), which stands out syntactically thanks to the shift of grammatical tense, is emphasized phonologically as well by the use of rhyme.

3.

We can tell from Szondi's annotations and corrections which specific points seemed important to him and on which observations he would have been likely to base his own reading of the poem.

(a) The word *Erde* ("earth") which has a special semantic link to the nine finite forms of the verb *graben* ("to dig") appears only once, in the first line of the poem; Szondi notes: "basically the key to the imagery [*Metaphorik*] of the poem as a whole."

(b) The distribution of the form *gruben* ("dug") over the first three stanzas: It appears at the end of the couplet, at the beginning of the second stanza, and at both the beginning and the end of the second quatrain. The last two instances frame a series of negations (*wurden nicht . . . kein . . . keinerlei*, "did not grow . . . no . . . no [sort of]") that, as in the first stanza (*lobten nicht*, "did not praise"), have a paratactic coordinating function.

(c) When the student mentions the identity of the inflectional morphemes in the third stanza, Szondi notes the "syntactical analogy" between the framed phrases (ll. 8 and 9) as well as the "semantic connection" between them (*sie wurden nicht weise, erfanden kein Lied,/erdachten sich keinerlei* Sprache, "they did not grow wise, invented no *song,*/thought up for themselves no *language*").

(d) In the fourth stanza, he gives particular importance to the characteristics that distinguish the third of the three syntactically (and also, Szondi notes, "in part lexically, and thus anaphorically") parallel phases that appear in the first two lines. While the first two phrases are linked by the use of alliteration (*Stille... Sturm,* "stillness ... storm"), the indefinite article, and the repetition of the verb in the same inflected form, the third segment is rendered weightier than the others by the use of the active subject, the definite article used in the plural (which governs the verb *kamen,* as opposed to *kam,* "came"), as well as the addition of the collective form *alle* ("all"). Szondi adds that this also sets up "an opposition."

(e) The variations described above and the movement of the two lines toward a climax put particular weight on the phrase *die Meere alle* ("all the oceans") that falls just before the caesura between lines 12 and 13 and emphasizes the opposition between them. At the same time, the parallel construction (*es kam* auch *ein Sturm* [11], *es gräbt* auch *der Wurm* [13]; "*and* there came a storm," "*and* the worm digs too") connects the two halves of the stanza and underlines the use of the definite article before *Wurm* (as opposed to the indefinite articles that appeared earlier). The last member in the sequence of nouns in stanza IV governed by definite articles (*die Meere* [12], *der Wurm* [13], *das Singende* [14], "that singing," or, literally, "what is singing") also stands in a particular semantic relationship to *Lied* ("song," 8) in stanza III.

(f) The reprise of the empty subject *es* in stanza IV points back to the first words of the poem. Szondi notes:

"Semantically as well ('*Erde*,' '*Meere*,' '*Sturm*' ['earth,' 'oceans,' 'storm']).'' His lexical comment apropos of the concrete relationship between the abstract noun *Stille* (11) and various elemental phenomena: "In '*Windstille*' ['calm,' 'no wind'], '*Meeresstille*' ['calm sea'], rarely stands alone."

(g) The interjection "o" appears four times before the pronominal forms in the first line of the last stanza, and the rhythm of line 15 leads up to a phonological shift from $o \rightarrow u$ (*o du*, "o you") at the end the line (cf. the repetition in line 17). In this context, Szondi points to the divergence of lines 5 and 6, which are identical except for their end words (*wollte* $\rightarrow$ *wußte* ["wanted" $\rightarrow$ "knew"]). In the distribution of the pronouns ("O one, o none, o no one, o you"), he sees both an opposition ($+ \quad - \quad - \quad +$) and, via these symmetrical antitheses, an intensification leading up to the final "you."

Szondi rejects the student's attempt to compare line 15 with the paradigmatic series of lines 13 (*Ich grabe, du gräbst*, "I dig, you dig . . . ") and 17, as if their individual elements were interchangeable. Rather, he insists on the difference between these lines, since lines 13 and 17 contain actual paradigms (in the verb conjugations), and the subjects in these series are predetermined, while in the sequence contained in line 15, what changes is "precisely the declared (potential) subjects," which stand doubly in opposition to one another, while, on the other hand, in both cases, the way in which "language asserts itself as a system" is apparent.

(h) Szondi was also interested in the use of rhyme in the last stanza, as well as the combined use of assonance (12/14) and rhyme in the penultimate stanza following the stanzas that are not rhymed. The assonance and rhyme are in turn prepared for by the use of alliteration (*ging*/*Gott* and *wollte/wußte*) in the second stanza, so that the poem itself appears to be finding its way to rhyme (*das Singende*) by way of assonance.

4.

The student presenting the interpretation finds—mistakenly, it would seem—that the poem makes relatively little use of phonetic equivalents. Szondi corrects this analysis, noting that the repetition of words is "an extreme form of 'equivalence'" and indeed entails reiterated sounds. Of the twelve forms of the verb *graben* ("to dig"), five of them, in lines 2, 3, 7 and 10, are in the preterit tense (*gruben*), whose "u" introduces a darker tonality, after which comes a transition to the present tense and the brighter vowels "a" (*grabe* [13], *graben* [14], *grab* [17]) and "ä" (*gräbt* [13], *gräbst* [17]), so that the opposition established between the two parts is reflected on the phonological level as well. That the poem's sounds become progressively brighter (moving from "o" to "u" to "i") is clearly evident when one examines the pattern not only of the rhyme words in the last two stanzas, but also the final stressed vowels in each of its lines:

1	*u*
2	*u*
3	i
4	o
5	o
6	*u*
7	e
8	i
9	a
10	*u*

```
11   u  ⎞
12   a  ⎟
13   u  ⎟⎞
14   a  ⎠

15   u  ⎞
16   i  ⎟                                    u
17   u  ⎟⎞                                   ↓
18   i  ⎠                                    i
```

The effect of brightening is intensified by the fact that, in addition to the "i" in lines 17 (*ich, ich, mich, dir*) and 18 (*Finger* and *Ring*), the darker vowels "o" and "u" appear five times in 17, but only twice in 18. The rhyme in lines 11/13 ("u") gives way to an even darker assonance, which in 15/17 in turn leads to the brighter vowel of *ging* (16, following 3) and *Ring* (18). Thus, the poem's phonological structure leads us to precisely the point indicated not only by the final metaphor of connection ("on our finger the ring awakes")—which involves the sole instance in the poem of the first person plural ("our") after all the appearances of the third person ("they")—but also, and above all, the verb "awakes," which transforms the poem's topos.

5.

There is a syntactical contrast between the two parts of the poem (1–12, 13–18), created above all through the exclusive use of the past tense in the first part and the present (with the exception of line 16) in the second. For Szondi, however, the most important difference is that "the introduction of the first person coincides" with the change of tense ("I dig"): "But far more important (than the disappearance of the pronoun 'they,' which appears eight times in the first section and once in the second) is that it is here that the 'I' is first introduced." Seen from the perspective of the rift between the sections, the first half of the stanza ("There came . . . , there came . . . / . . . came") concludes a first phase and appears "as a conclusion, but as one that paradoxically tears the two parts asunder."

Just as the poem progressively discovers rhyme, it gradually proceeds from third-person narration to the use of the first and second persons, whereby the language itself, asserting itself in the form of "systems" (13 and 17 in the scheme of conjugations, 15 in the sequence of pronouns), produces the "I" and the "you."

While in the first part, the words taken from the semantic field of speaking, of speech, appear only in negated form ("did not praise" [4], "invented no song" [8]), by the end of the poem, it can be said affirmatively of *das Singende* itself that it "out there says: They dig" [14]. In the distance, "out there" (*dort*), *das Singende* can be understood as a designation for precisely the "narrated" part of the poem, which is determined by the third person plural and the past tense ("narrated" according to Weinrich's terminology, as opposed to the "spoken world" of the second part).[3]

The use of the verb *graben* (referring to "earth") in the second series of forms reveals, semantically as well as phonetically, the transition (to "I" and "you") and the reversal. One might at first suppose that these forms using "a" and "ä" were pointing to a different action that hasn't yet begun. But in reality, this modification indicates that the "telos" has been reached.

6.

Thus, there is a "connection between the two halves" in which "the 'they' of the first half is more precisely determined by the 'I' and 'you' of the second." This is supported by "the digging of the 'they' and the digging of the 'I' (and the 'you')."

While at the beginning of the poem one can at most surmise that the "they" refers, in accordance with a "poetic tradition," to a pair of lovers, this assumption becomes a certainty on the basis of the topos reflected in the poem's last line.

In the middle of the present-tense section, not only the past tense, but also the impersonal subject (from lines 1 and 11/12) are reprised (in line 16), which makes the question appear to be a retrospective "glance back" to the first part. These discrepancies accentuate the hiatus that separates the question being posed about what direction there is amid the lack of direction from the specification that follows, since the next line (by contrast) picks up once more the result of the pronoun series in line 15 ("o you") and alters the paradigm of line 13. In the course of the scheme of conjugations (this time: "you" and "I"), the "I" and the "you" are finally introduced, which in a sense already answers the question: A link is being established that goes beyond mere juxtaposition, and thus the direction for the digging is specified (Szondi's note: "*ich grab mich dir zu* ['I dig towards you']" but in the preterit: "*da's nirgendhin ging* ['when it led nowhere']").

(During the seminar session, Szondi is said to have compared the "retrospective" moment in the poem before the telos is reached with the fourth movement of Beethoven's Ninth Symphony, in which various earlier themes, in particular the "terror fanfare," are revisited just before the "Ode to Joy."[4] Szondi concluded that, in the poem as in the symphony, there is "no problematization of the synthesis," which is in both cases problematic.)

Szondi explains the small number of nouns as being not so much (as his student suggested) a shying away from giving names to things as arising "because the only matter being discussed is what takes place between an I and a you."

Appendix C
Notes on "Blume"

The first of Szondi's two pages of notes on the linguistic analysis of the poem "Blume" (Flower) maps out the correspondences between lexical, metaphorical, and phonetic/phonological readings of the poem as well as providing a prosodic analysis. These four systems are recorded in four different colors on a single copy of the poem. Of the five columns Szondi drew in the margin, only one has been filled out, indicating the person and number of each of the personal and possessive pronouns. On the second page, the prosodic analysis of the poem is repeated, with each of the lines divided into feet and labeled "f" (*fallend*—for falling meter) or "st" (*steigend*—rising meter) in the margin. These notes were to have guided Szondi in his work on the essay; only in a few areas can we predict what form his interpretation might have taken.

BLUME

1 Der Stein.
2 Der Stein in der Luft, dem ich folgte.
3 Dein Aug, so blind wie der Stein.

4 Wir waren
5 Hände,
6 wir schöpften die Finsternis leer, wir fanden
7 das Wort, das den Sommer heraufkam:
8 Blume.

9 Blume—ein Blindenwort.
10 Dein Aug und mein Aug:
11 sie sorgen
12 für Wasser.

13 Wachstum.
14 Herzwand um Herzwand
15 blättert hinzu.

16 Ein Wort noch, wie dies, und die Hämmer
17 schwingen im Freien.

FLOWER

1 The stone.
2 The stone in the air, which I followed.
3 Your eye, as blind as the stone.

4 We were
5 hands,
6 we baled the darkness empty, we found
7 the word that ascended summer:
8 flower.

9 Flower—a blind man's word.
10 Your eye and mine:
11 they see
12 to water.

13 Growth.
14 Heart wall upon heart wall
15 adds petals to it.

16 One more word like this, and the hammers
17 will swing over open ground.[1]

(a) *Lexically*, only the iterations are recorded: exclusively nouns and pronouns. No verbs or adjectives are repeated, and in fact the poem contains almost no adjectives and not many verbs: there are only 8 verbs to 21 nouns (that is, 14 plus repetitions):

1. *Stein*	("stone"),	1 – 2 – 3.
2. *Dein*	("your"),	3 – 10.
3. *Aug*	("eye"),	3 – 10 – 10.
4. *blind*	("blind"),	3 – 9.
5. *Wir*	("we"),	4 – 6 – 6.
6. Wort	("word"),	7 – 9 – 16.
7. *Blume*	("flower"),	8 – 9.
8. *Herzwand*	("heart wall"),	14 – 14.

(b) The following words are *metaphorically* linked:

1. "hands" (5) – "baled" (6) – "empty" (6);
2. "flower" (9) – "water" (12) – "growth" (13) – "adds petals to it" (15);
3. "wall . . . wall" (14, in: "heart wall") – "hammers" (16) – "swing" (17); and also:
4. "wall" (14) – "(over) open ground" (17).

(c) If one follows the *phonetic/phonological* links involving the initial "bl" on the one hand, as in:

blind ("blind," 3), *Blume* ("flower," 8), *Blume* (9), *Blinden(wort)* ("blind man's [word]," 9), *blättert* ("adds petals," 15),

and on the other hand, the instances of the sound "wo-/wa-" in:

Wort ("word," 7), *(Blinden)wort* (9), *Wasser* ("water," 12), *Wachstum* ("growth," 13), *(Herz)wand,*

(Herz)wand ("[heart] wall," 14), *Wort . . . wie* ("word like," 16),[2]

it becomes clear that both these series are distributed among both halves of the poem, but intersect in the compound *Blindenwort*; line 9, the first line of the third stanza, therefore, constitutes the center of the poem, not only numerically, but also in terms of this relationship. The two parts are also dovetailed: One element of each series extends beyond this point of intersection (*Wort* appears already in 7, *blättert* still in 15) and thus has an anticipatory or reiterative function. Viewed in the light of this structure, the double repetition of the title "Blume" at the poem's center (in two successive lines, at the end of the second stanza and the beginning of the third) appears all the more significant, especially as "flower" is specific to this particular poem, while the words "stone," "eye," "blind," "heart," and "word" appear repeatedly through- out the volume *Sprachgitter*. (A comparison with the other poems in the collection allows us to see the *Aug* as distant and dead and suggests the convergence of "Your eye" [3] and "The stone" [2], thereby also determining the identity of the "we" [6].)[3] The link with "blind" shows the word *Blume* to be rising up from the realm of the dead; at the same time, as "word," giving life to itself, it overcomes the coming to life of the "remembered." (Of all the repetitions in the poem, those of "word," which frame much more of the poem than its central lines [9–10], stand out.)

(d) This division in the poem is also reflected in the dis- tribution of the pronouns: The "I" (2) and the "Your" (3) in the first part of the poem are subsumed under the "we," which is repeated twice. The "we" appears as a subject (in which the persons remain present: "We were/hands" [4/5] "we . . . we" [6]), while the "I" is later represented by a second eye ("and mine [my eye]," [10]), and the "I" and "you" together are objectified as independent subjects, through the "they" (the eyes).

(e) This division can also be seen in the contrasting rhythmical elements. In the first two stanzas, all the lines are characterized by rising meter (iambic and anapestic): *dem ich folgte* (∪ ∪ — | ∪) ("which I followed"), *wir waren* (∪ — | ∪) ("we were"), and so forth, with the exception of the two lines that consist only of a word without an article, the predicate *Hände* (5) and the object *Blume* (8). These single-word lines anticipate the almost consistently falling meter (trochaic and dactylic) of the second part of the poem:[4] for instance, *Blume— ein Blindenwort* (— ∪ ∪ | — ∪ ∪) and *Dein Aug und mein Aug* (— ∪ ∪ | — ∪).

The strongly accented words *Hände* and *Blume* (which appeared already in the poem's title) stand here as the result of the activity concentrated around them. In the right-hand margin of the prosodic analysis, Szondi lists four words separately: in the title *Blume* (— ∪), then *Der Stein* (∪ —), *Hände* (— ∪), and finally *Blume* (— ∪). The two one-word lines, which are marked with asterisks in the analyzed text, point to the expanded version (also marked with an asterisk) of the same falling metrical pattern at the end of the poem: *schwingen im Freien* (— ∪ ∪ | — ∪). If we also take into account the single non-asyndetic locution in the poem (*und die Hämmer,* "and the hammers," 16), this shows that intensification and decay are not mutually exclusive, and that the ambiguity of the future has not been resolved.

Notes

Foreword

1. Yet another plan for the volume (probably made shortly before Szondi decided to proceed with *Celan-Studien*) even includes the essay "Reading 'Engführung.'"

2. Celan had been accused by Claire Goll, the widow of poet Yvan Goll, whose work Celan had translated, of plagiarizing Goll in his own poems—SB.

3. Szondi later (summer semester 1967) included "Engführung" in a seminar on the hermetic poem (Mallarmé, Eliot, Celan), Celan's translation of Shakespeare's Sonnet 2 (summer semester 1969) in an introductory course on the methods of comparative literature, and "Es war Erde in ihnen" in a seminar on the linguistic analysis of poems. [See also the notes on "Es war Erde in ihnen" in Appendix B—SB.]

4. A second table of contents on the same page lists only four chapters: (1) "Engführung," (2) "Constancy," (3) "Erde," (4) "Eden."

5. Szondi's notebook contains the titles he considered for the essay: "Beständigkeit des Verses" (The constancy of [the] verse), "Geborgener Vers" (Borrowed verse).

6. *Neue Zürcher Zeitung*, November 19, 1960; see also *Neue Deutsche Hefte* 78, January 1961.

The Poetry of Constancy

1. William Shakespeare, *Einundzwanzig Sonette* (Twenty-one sonnets), trans. Paul Celan (Frankfurt am Main: Insel, 1967), 35.

2. William Shakespeare, *The Sonnets*, ed. John Dover Wilson (Cambridge: Cambridge University Press, 1966), 55.

3. Letter of April 2, 1804 to Friedrich Wilmans. [Friedrich Hölderlin, *Sämtliche Werke*, vol. 6.1, ed. Friedrich Beissner (Stuttgart: Kohlhammer, 1954), 439—SB.]

4. Sonnet 104, l.1.

5. Charles Baudelaire, *Tableaux Parisiens*, German trans. with a preface, "Die Aufgabe des Übersetzers," by Walter Benjamin (Heidelberg: Weissbach, 1923), reprinted in Walter Benjamin, *Gesammelte Schriften*, vol. 4:1, ed. Tilman Rexroth (Frankfurt am Main: Suhrkamp, 1972), 9–21; ["The Task of the Translator," in *Illuminations*, trans. Harry Zohn (New York: Harcourt, Brace, and World, 1968), 69–82—SB.]

In Benjamin's essay, "intention" (*Intention*) does not mean "purpose" (*Absicht*). What Benjamin means can perhaps best be understood from the following passage from Fritz Mauthner: "Throughout the Middle Ages the concept of *intentio* did not [apply] to the will, but rather to knowing, or to the energy or tension involved in knowing. The Schoolmen's Latin was bad, and in *intentio* they could still detect the original meaning, the metaphor of the taut bow and the aiming of the arrow; hence for them *intentio* was directedness of attention or of consciousness to a perceived or perceptible object." F. Mauthner, *Wörterbuch der Philosophie: Neue Beiträge zu einer Kritik der Sprache*, vol. 1 (Munich: G. Müller, 1910), 584–85. In the following discussion, the concept of "intention toward language" is not used strictly in Benjamin's sense, insofar as it has been divorced from the theoretical background of Benjamin's views on language and contains ideas deriving from modern linguistics. For our present purposes, "intention toward language" may be defined as the directedness of consciousness toward language, that is, as the linguistic conception preceding all speech; in other words, it may be seen as the mode of signification that stamps linguistic usage.

6. Benjamin, "The Task of the Translator."

7. Michel Foucault, *Les mots et les choses* (Paris: Gallimard, 1966). [*The Order of Things* (New York: Vintage, 1973). "Words and things" is the literal translation of the title—SB.]

8. See Peter Szondi, "Über philologische Erkenntnis," *Hölderlin-Studien* (Frankfurt am Main: Suhrkamp, 1970), 22. ["On Textual Understanding," in *On Textual Understanding and Other Essays*, trans. Harvey Mendelson (Minneapolis: University of Minnesota Press, 1986), 13: "Historicity is in fact a part of its [the individual work's] particularity, so that the *only* approach that does full justice to the work of art is the one that allows us to see history in the work of art, not the one that shows us the work of art in history"—SB.]

9. An analysis of Shakespeare's sonnet that would do justice to it would have to proceed from its own distinctive features, but that would carry us beyond the bounds of the present essay.

10. See Jacques Derrida, "La double séance," *Tel Quel* 41 (spring 1970) and 42 (summer 1970); reprinted in *La dissémination* (Paris: Seuil, 1972), 199–321. ["The Double Session," *Disseminations*, trans. Barbara Johnson (Chicago: University of Chicago Press, 1981), 173–366—SB.]

11. See Michel Deguy, "Vers une théorie de la figure généralisée," *Critique* 269 (October 1969).

12. Cf. Heinrich Lausberg, *Handbuch der literarischen Rhetorik* (Munich: Hueber, 1960), 361.

13. Stefan George, *Werke*, vol. 2 (Munich: Küpper, 1958), 203.

14. Cf. Theodor W. Adorno, *Negative Dialektik* (Frankfurt am Main: Suhrkamp, 1966), 156ff. [*Negative Dialectics*, trans. E. B. Ashton (New York: Seabury, 1973)—SB.] See also "Parataxis: Zur späten Lyrik Hölderlins," in *Noten zur Literatur*, vol. 3 (Frankfurt am Main: Suhrkamp, 1965), 184. [Reprinted in *Gesammelte Schriften*, vol. 11, ed. Rolf Tiedemann (Frankfurt am Main: Suhrkamp, 1974). "Parataxis: On Hölderlin's Late Poetry," in

Notes to Literature, vol. 2, trans Sherry Weber Nicholsen (New York: Columbia University Press, 1992)—SB.]

15. Cf. Benjamin, "The Task of the Translator."

16. Alexander Schmidt, *Shakespeare-Lexicon*, vol. 2, 5th ed. (Berlin: de Gruyter, 1962), 1310.

17. Gerald Willen and Victor B. Reed, eds., *A Casebook on Shakespeare's Sonnets* (New York: Crowell, 1964), 107.

18. Paul Celan, "Es war Erde in ihnen," *Die Niemandsrose* (Frankfurt am Main: S. Fischer, 1963), 9. ["There was earth inside them," *Poems of Paul Celan*, trans. Michael Hamburger (New York: Persea, 1980), 153, trans. modified—HM.]

19. The English text printed in the volume was not suggested by Celan, nor did he provide the publisher with it; he did, however, examine and approve it. (This information was kindly given me by Klaus Reichert.)

20. See Jacques Derrida, "La double séance," and also his "Sémiologie et grammatologie," *Information sur les sciences sociales* 7, no. 3 (1968) (Recherches Sémiotiques). [Reprinted in *Positions* (Paris: Minuit, 1972), 25–50; *Positions*, trans. Alan Bass (Chicago: University of Chicago Press, 1981), 15–36—SB.]

21. See note 26.

22. It would be worthwhile to examine the function of this program (or experiment) of a poetics of constancy in Celan's own poetry and in its development.

23. See note 19.

24. See the reference in note 14. In Hölderlin, to be sure, parataxis serves to isolate individual words, whereas in Celan, at least in this translation, it pertains more to the relationship of the lines and sentences. In Celan's own poetry, parataxis involving individual words plays a decisive role.

25. See note 19. The typographical separation of the quatrains was probably made in order to have the corresponding lines of the original and the translation face each other in the dual language edition.

26. Roman Jakobson, "Linguistics and Poetics," in *Style in*

Language, ed. Thomas A. Sebeok (Cambridge, Mass.: Technology Press of MIT, 1960), 358. In the poetic sequence, the equivalences correspond to the passage of time. It is perhaps no accident that sonnets are the subject both of Jakobson's most important interpretations of poems and of the present essay: "Le sonnet est fait pour le simultané. Quatorze vers *simultanés*, et fortement désignés comme tels par l'enchaînement et la conservation des rimes: type et structure d'un poème *stationnaire*." Paul Valéry, *Tel Quel*, in *Oeuvres*, vol. 2 (Paris: Pléiade, 1960), 676. ("The sonnet is made for the simultaneous. Fourteen *simultaneous* verses, and vigorously designated as such by the linking and conserving of rhymes: type and structure of a *stationary* poem"— trans. Andrzej Warminski.) In the framework of Jakobson's definition of the "poetic function," the conjugation paradigm, which was discussed in connection with the passages *was ich da treib und trieb* and *Ich find, erfind*, turns out to be a special case of what modern linguistics terms "paradigmatics."

27. The present essay is concerned with Celan's intention toward language. It should be complemented by an analysis of his way of fashioning language. Such an analysis would have to devote particular attention to the expressive value and tone of turns of phrase like *den ich da lieb, was ich da treib*, and *all dieses Singen*. It would show that with these linguistic means, Celan expresses not only the contemplative distance of the melancholic to himself and to the object of his love—and the "I" who speaks in Shakespeare's sonnets may rightly be termed a melancholic—but also the distance between himself and the subjective dimension as such, from which Celan turns away in favor of the objectivity of the poem, which is concerned only with itself. This objectivity is established by a language that, like the one examined here, no longer serves the function of representation. Yet, in the final line (*In Einem will ich drei zusammenschmieden*), intense light falls on the "I" that sets itself this task, in opposition not only to the "I" standing behind the veil of melancholy, an "I" that lives *there* (*da*), but also to the programmatic objectivity of the poem.

Reading "Engführung"

1. This sentence has been shortened in the present translation of Szondi's essay; it is the first of several brief passages devoted specifically to the French translation of Celan's poem. All such passages have been elided in the main text, but preserved in this and the following notes. Szondi writes here, discussing the poem's opening lines in Jean Daive's translation:

> Dé-
> porté dans
> l'étendue
> à la trace sans faille:
> . . .
> Herbe, écrite: désassemblée. Les pierres, blanches,
> et l'ombre des tiges:

"The French version by Jean Daive, which Daive certainly discussed with Celan himself, is less ambiguous here than the German text. The masculine past participle (*déporté*) prevents a reading that is grammatically possible in the German: that the grass itself, this *Gras, auseinandergeschrieben*, is what has been deported to the *Gelände mit der untrüglichen Spur*. This is not the reading we would have preferred had we been reading the poem in the German original. But it is a possible reading nonetheless." Daive's translation appeared first in *L'Ephémère* 4, then in *Strette*, trans. André du Bouchet, Jean-Pierre Burgart, and Jean Daive (Paris: Mercure de France, 1971)—SB.

2. Speaking again of Jean Daive's translation, Szondi writes: "The translation suppresses this ambiguity, which does not at all mean—let's establish this once and for all—that the translation authorized by the poet shows us the correct meaning of the text, which the ambiguity of the original kept us from ascertaining. The suppression of the polysemy eliminates the ambiguity, which is neither a defect nor purely a stylistic trait, and which determines the structure of the poetic text itself"—SB.

3. The expression "imaginary universe" refers to the title of

the book by Jean-Pierre Richard, *L'univers imaginaire de Mallarmé* (Paris: Seuil, 1961)—JB.

4. Cf. Jacques Derrida, "La double séance," *Tel Quel* 42 (spring 1970), 20ff. [Reprinted in *La dissémination* (Paris: Seuil, 1972), 199–321; "The Double Session," *Disseminations*, trans. Barbara Johnson (Chicago: University of Chicago Press, 1981), 173–336—SB.]

5. Szondi's argument in this paragraph is influenced by the French translation of *zuhause* ("at home"): *de retour* ("back at home," "having returned home"), which he understands as implying motion, certainly more than in the German text. I have interpolated "The region to which one is returning so as to be 'at home'" (*L'endroit où l'on est "de retour"*). Throughout this passage, then, the words "at home" should be understood as (also) implying motion in the direction of home—SB.

6. Rather than the *OED*, Szondi cites two definitions for "stretto" from French sources: it is "the section of a fugue in which the theme appears only in fragments and which resembles an intense, urgent dialogue" (*Littré*); the section in which "theme and response chase one another, with the entrances coming at increasingly short intervals" (*Robert*)—SB.

7. In the corresponding sentence in Szondi's original, he comments on the normalizing translation of *redeten von/Worten* as *prononcèrent/des paroles*: "It is certain that in this stanza the translation, which combines beauty with the greatest precision, neglects, perhaps necessarily, two important nuances. In the original text, it is not said that they *prononcèrent/des paroles*, 'pronounced words,' but that they spoke of words, or even that they 'talked words' (*redeten von/Worten*)." Later in the paragraph (where I have interpolated: "Also ambiguous is the pronoun *keines*"), Szondi turns to the second lost nuance: "In addition, when the translator (having had no other choice in this case) uses the pronoun *nul* in the feminine (*Nulle ne/s'éveilla*), although it is neuter in the German, the ambiguity is lost. In the text, the pronoun *keines* can refer both to the words and to those who pronounce them"—SB.

8. Szondi here criticizes the French translation. "The French expression *je vous donnai l'alarme* seems, on first reading, not to correspond to the German text: *ich tickte euch zu.*" Later in the paragraph, speaking of the two meanings of the verb *ticken*, he adds: "This ambiguity has not escaped the translator. In translating one of the two senses of *ticken* as 'to sound an alarm' (not a meaning of *ticken*), he has succeeded in evoking the bell, another emblem of time"—SB.

9. Szondi adds "by the prosodic device of enjambment, which does not respect the unity of the word (*Le re-/couvrit— qui?*)." A line break in the middle of a word such as appears in the French translation of this line does not occur at this point in the original text (*Deckte es/zu—wer?*), though examples of such enjambment can be found elsewhere in the poem, e.g., *ver-/ästelt* (VI)—SB.

10. This interpretation, which follows the French translation of the poem here and elsewhere, does not mention the rhyme between *leuchten* ("to shine") and *feuchten* ("moist"). In a conversation with one of his students, Szondi once mentioned that the German version of his essay would take this mediation into account—JB.

11. Cf. Dante, *Inferno* (canto 5, line 138): *quel giorno più non vi leggemmo avante* ("that day we read no more"). Celan referred several times to this "source" for the passage of "Engführung" *wir /lasens im Buche*—JB.

12. Diogenes Laertius, IX, 44.

13. The German *er* ("he") can also mean "it" when referring to a masculine noun, in this case *der Stein*, "the stone"—SB.

14. Stéphane Mallarmé, "Crise de vers" (Crisis of poetry), *Oeuvres complètes* (Paris: Gallimard-Pléiade, 1945), 336: *s'allument de reflets réciproques comme une virtuelle traînée de feux sur des pierreries.*

15. Szondi introduces this sentence as a comment on the translation of the stanza:

> Fusa, fusa.
> Puis—

Nuits, démêlées. Cercles
verts ou bleus, carrés
rouges: le
monde s'engage
dans le jeu avec les heures
nouvelles. —Cercles,
rouges ou noirs, carrés
lumineux, nulle
ombre de vol,
nulle
table, nulle
âme en fumée ne monte ni ne prend part au jeu.

"As in the case of *ticken*, the translator, an admirable reader of 'Engführung,' was on several occasions able to find ingenious methods for recreating in the French version this language, by definition untranslatable, in which the words to which the poet has ceded the initiative 'illumine one another with reciprocal reflections like a virtual streak of flame upon jewels.' For one thing, the word that expresses the mode of action by which the world is being created: *fuser* (*anschiessen*) recalls *fusil, fusiller* (*schiessen*), which is suggested by the *paraballe* (*Kugelfang*) in section VIII and whose importance will soon become evident"—SB.

16. A *Meßtisch* is the instrument known in English as a plane table: "A surveying instrument used for measuring angles in mapping, consisting of a circular drawing-table mounted horizontally on a tripod, and having an alidade pivoted over its centre" (*Oxford English Dictionary*, 2d ed., 1989), but the word, literally "measuring table," also calls up associations with *Messe* ("mass") and tailors' shops—SB.

17. *Almanach de la Librairie Flinker* (Paris, 1958), 45.

18. Cf. Jacques Derrida, "Sémiologie et grammatologie," *Information sur les sciences sociales* 7, no. 3 (1968) (Recherches sémiotiques). [Reprinted in *Positions* (Paris: Minuit, 1972), 25–50; *Positions*, trans. Alan Bass (Chicago: University of Chicago Press, 1981), 15–36—SB.]

19. One of the few examples given in the Grimms' dictionary is by the novelist Celander (1685–1735).

20. Of the French line *Sur la/lèpre pétrifiée*, Szondi writes: "the French expression is obscure, since we cannot know why 'leprosy' is at issue here or what we should make of the fact that it is 'petrified.' But at the same time, this expression is the clearest 'sign' of the mediation that unites the organic with the inorganic universe: leprosy has become stone. Nonetheless, the two questions we have just posed call for a response. Unfortunately, this response is given only by the German text, whose ambiguity could not be captured in the French version. *Aussatz*, which means 'leprosy,' does not mean only that"—SB.

21. Szondi writes: "*Dans/l'ultime éversion*—in German: *in/der jüngsten Verwerfung*. We must admit we do not understand the choice of words in the French. (We admit this not without hesitation, since Celan most probably accepted this translation.) Although the term *éversion* ("overthrow") is appropriate for setting up the last line of this stanza (*devant/le mur éboulé*) and was perhaps selected for this reason, it is certain that in German it is not a question of *éversion*, but of rejection, reprobation. So the *jüngste Verwerfung* cannot signify anything other than the fate to which millions of Jews were subjected during the Nazi era, among them the parents of the poet, the last of the reprobations that have been inflicted on the people of Israel since the beginning of their history"—SB.

22. Theodor W. Adorno, "Kulturkritik und Gesellschaft" (written 1949), in *Prismen: Kulturkritik und Gesellschaft* (Frankfurt am Main: Suhrkamp, 1955), 31. [*Prisms*, trans. Samuel and Shierry Weber (Cambridge, Mass.: MIT Press, 1983)—SB]—JB.

23. Cf. Theodor W. Adorno, *Negative Dialektik* (Frankfurt am Main: Suhrkamp, 1966), 353. [*Negative Dialectics*, trans. E. B. Ashton (New York: Seabury, 1973)—SB.]

Eden

1. Paul Celan, *Schneepart* (Snow part) (Frankfurt am Main: Suhrkamp, 1971), 8.

2. *Hommage für Peter Huchel, zum 3. April 1968*, ed. Otto F. Best (Munich: Piper, 1968), 16.

3. Paul Celan, *Ausgewählte Gedichte* (Selected poems), ed. Klaus Reichert (Frankfurt am Main: Suhrkamp, 1970), 167.

4. I am indebted to Klaus Reichert for this information.

5. The lines *Ein blatt, baumlos/für Bertolt Brecht* (*Schneepart*, 59) would be a title for the variation on a Brecht poem that follows them were it not for adjective and colon. ["A leaf, treeless/ for Bertolt Brecht": trans. Michael Hamburger, *Poems of Paul Celan* (New York: Persea, 1980), 287—SB.]

6. Cf. "La contrescarpe," l. 29–32: *Über Krakau/bist du gekommen, am Anhalter/Bahnhof/floß deinen Blicken ein Rauch zu. Die Niemandsrose* (The no one's rose) (Frankfurt am Main: S. Fischer, 1963), 81. ["Via Cracow/you came, at the Anhalter/ Station/smoke flowed toward your gaze."—SB.]

7. On July 20, 1944, Colonel Claus Schenk von Stauffenberg had led an unsuccessful attempt to assassinate Hitler—SB.

8. *Der Mord an Rosa Luxemburg und Karl Liebknecht: Dokumentation eines politischen Verbrechens* (The murder of Rosa Luxemburg and Karl Liebknecht: Documentation of a political crime), ed. Elisabeth Hannover-Drück and Heinrich Hannover (Frankfurt am Main: Suhrkamp, 1967).

9. Ibid., 99.

10. Ibid., 129.

11. This nocturnal drive provides the background for the collection's second Berlin poem, *"Lila luft mit gelben Fensterflecken," Schneepart*, 9. ("Purple air with yellow window patches.")

12. Cf. "Todesfuge," *Mohn und Gedächtnis* (Poppy and memory) (Stuttgart: Deutsche Verlags-Anstalt, 1952), 37. ["Death Fugue," trans. Michael Hamburger, *Poems of Paul Celan*, 50–52 —SB.]

13. Cf. Roman Jakobson and Morris Halle, *Fundamentals of Language, Part 2* (The Hague: Mouton, 1956).

14. Cf. *Daselbst wurde ihm der Kopf abgehauen und auf den Staken gesetzt* ("And there his head was chopped off and placed

upon a stake") G. Freytag, quoted in Grimm, *Deutsches Wörter-buch* (German dictionary), s.v. *Staken.*

Appendix A

1. Karl Kraus, *Worte in Versen* (Words in verse), *Werke* 7 (Munich: Kösel, 1959).

Appendix B

1. This essay appeared in *L'Homme: Revue française d'anthropologie* II, no. 1 (1962), 5–21, and in German translation in *Sprache im technischen Zeitalter* 29 (1969), 2–19. English translation in *The Structuralists from Marx to Lévi-Strauss*, ed. Richard T. De George and Fernande M. De George (Garden City, N.Y.: Doubleday, 1972).

2. Paul Celan, *Die Niemandsrose* (The no one's rose) (Frankfurt am Main: S. Fischer, 1963), 9. *Poems of Paul Celan*, trans. Michael Hamburger (New York: Persea, 1980), 131.

3. Harald Weinrich, *Tempus—Besprochene und erzählte Welt*, (Stuttgart: Kohlhammer, 1964).

4. In German, the opening of the symphony's fourth movement is commonly referred to as the *Schreckensfanfare* ("terror fanfare")—SB.

Appendix C

1. Paul Celan, *Sprachgitter* (Speech grille*)* (Frankfurt am Main: S. Fischer, 1959), 25. *Poems of Paul Celan*, trans. Michael Hamburger (New York: Persea, 1980), 99.

2. While *wie* (16) is attached to *Wort* (*ein Wort noch, wie dies*), the *wie* of *wie der Stein* (3), *wir waren* (4), and the repetition of *wir* (6) do not form part of this phonological pattern.

3. It is important to remember that these notes are an expansion by Jean Bollack of Szondi's notes on "Blume" and do not

necessarily reflect Szondi's intentions in every detail. This particular suggestion violates the argument presented by Szondi in "Reading 'Engführung'" that it is illegitimate to explain a difficult line in a poem by quoting other works by the same author in which the same words appear—though the contradiction may also have been Szondi's own—SB.

4. Szondi noted *st* (for *steigend*, rising meter) in the margin beside lines 11 and 12, but the metrical analysis ($\cup\,|-\cup$) reveals falling meter here (and not [$\cup-|\cup$] as in *wir waren*, 4). The penultimate line is labeled only with a question mark, as if Szondi were undecided between the two interpretations ($-\,-|\cup\,\cup-|\cup\,\cup-|\cup$) and ($-\,|-\cup\,\cup\,|-\cup\,\cup|-\cup$).

MERIDIAN

Crossing Aesthetics

Emmanual Levinas, *God, Death, and Time*

Ernst Bloch, *The Spirit of Utopia*

Giorgio Agamben, *Potentialities: Collected Essays in Philosophy*

Ellen S. Burt, *Poetry's Appeal: French Nineteenth-Century Lyric and the Political Space*

Jacques Derrida, *Adieu to Emmanuel Levinas*

Werner Hamacher, *Premises: Essays on Philosophy and Literature from Kant to Celan*

Aris Fioretos, *The Gray Book*

Deborah Esch, *In the Event: Reading Journalism, Reading Theory*

Winfried Menninghaus, *In Praise of Nonsense: Kant and Bluebeard*

Giorgio Agamben, *The Man Without Content*

Giorgio Agamben, *The End of the Poem: Essays in Poetics*

Theodor W. Adorno, *Sound Figures*

Louis Marin, *Sublime Poussin*

Philippe Lacoue-Labarthe, *Poetry as Experience*

Ernst Bloch, *Literary Essays*

Jacques Derrida, *Resistances of Psychoanalysis*

Marc Froment-Meurice, *That Is to Say: Heidegger's Poetics*

Francis Ponge, *Soap*

Philippe Lacoue-Labarthe, *Typography: Mimesis, Philosophy, Politics*